KENT
OF M
AND MURDER

———— ✿ ————

W. H. Johnson

COUNTRYSIDE BOOKS
NEWBURY, BERKSHIRE

COUNTRYSIDE BOOKS
3 Catherine Road
Newbury, Berkshire

To view our complete range of books,
please visit us at
www.countrysidebooks.co.uk

ISBN 1 85306 810 1

Produced through MRM Associates Ltd., Reading
Typeset by Techniset Typesetters, Newton-le-Willows
Printed by J. W. Arrowsmith Ltd., Bristol

Contents

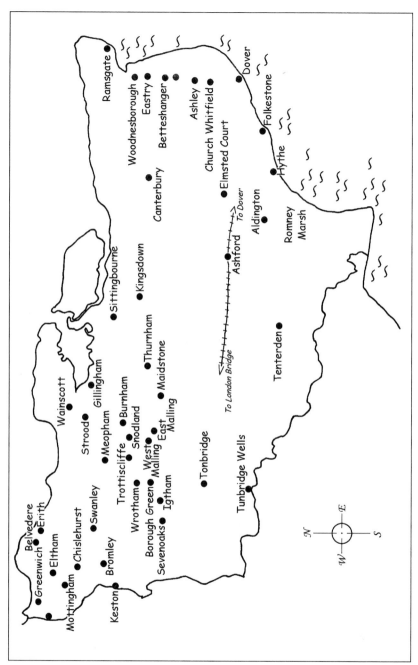

MAP OF THE COUNTY OF KENT

INTRODUCTION

In this collection of mysteries and murders I hope that there is enough new material to intrigue the reader. Certainly at least ten of the tales have never before appeared in book form.

Among the murderers, in addition to an education officer and a doctor, I have found space for a soldier, Gunner Buckfield, one of Britain's oddest killers, who, while in a police cell, wrote what he claimed to be a fictitious account of a murder. It was no more than a description of the appalling crime that he had carried out only hours before.

Then I thought some unsolved murders would be interesting. I could not omit the silent victim, Margery Wren, and poor Simon Law, whose killers will never now be brought to justice. And I have included the intriguing murder of Jane Clousen and the better known Luard case, both of which continue to puzzle criminologists. In addition I have come right up to the year 2000 with an account of a gangster execution in an Ashford car park. Each of these tales has a powerful narrative drive.

As for the mysteries, I thought it important to include an account of the Great Bullion Robbery. It surely must have a place in the annals of Kent mystery, as one of the most fascinating criminal enterprises. One ought not to praise criminals, although in this case one cannot but admire their skill. Sadly, some years ago, Hollywood got hold of the story and botched it, misrepresenting both the events and the characters.

I felt that I could not ignore the fascinating subject of ley lines. If my chapter does no more than encourage readers to get out their maps and perhaps their walking shoes, it will have served its purpose.

Perhaps the most contentious mystery here deals with alien

abduction. You don't believe in it? You don't think it possible? That's not the point. Some people do believe in it and its possibility, and this is their story.

This has been a most interesting book to work on. I only hope that readers will find it equally interesting to read.

Johnnie Johnson

Acknowledgements

I am very grateful to those who have been able to offer me help with this book. I should like in particular to thank Maureen Fearn of the North West Kent Family History Society and Paul Williams, a former curator of the Black Museum, who through his Murder Files provides me with all sorts of invaluable material. My old friend David Orchard has also, as ever, played his part.

It would be remiss to ignore the wonderful Kent Library Services and of course the Centre for Kentish Studies. The staff at Eastbourne Central Library have also, as ever, been very helpful.

Finally, my thanks go to my wife, Anne, for her sorely tried patience and for her valuable commentary on each of the chapters.

To any whose copyright I have failed to trace may I apologise in advance. Any omission will be amended in future printings.

A VERY PUBLIC EXECUTION

———————— ❈ ————————

Strange what witnesses say they have heard or seen – but of course, sometimes after a dramatic event the mind does play tricks. For instance two of the witnesses in the car park thought they heard the man call out, 'Please don't kill me. Please don't shoot.' But it is really extremely unlikely there was such a plea. Alan Decabral probably never saw the man who appeared at the window of the black Peugeot 206 at the Warren Retail Park in Ashford. Nor is it likely that he saw the pistol or heard the shot which was fired into the side of his head. This was a professional execution, quick and efficient. The assassin had waited for his opportunity, had probably followed his victim from his Pluckley home and watched while Decabral's partner, Susan Quinn, left the car outside Halfords to go shopping while the victim stayed in the passenger seat awaiting her return.

There was a bustle about the car park that Thursday, 6th October 2000. It was full at 1.30 pm – car boots opening and closing, trolleys rattling, mothers with their pushchairs, pensioners heavily laden – such ordinary, everyday surroundings for such a brutal slaying.

Even if some of those present unconsciously embellished their stories, several people were able to give a description of the killer: young – early twenties, perhaps – wearing a light green jacket, and they had seen him running away, they said. But even today the police have not yet tracked down the man who put that single bullet in Alan Decabral's untidy mane.

When the news of Decabral's murder was announced on the news, few perhaps recalled his name, unusual though it is. But then, when pictures of the murdered man appeared on their TV screens, many did remember him. He was too distinctive to forget. Only a year or so earlier he had had some fleeting fame as one of the principal witnesses in the M25 'road rage' murder case, when Kenneth Noye, one of Britain's most feared gangsters, had received a life sentence for stabbing 21-year-old Stephen Cameron on a slip-road at Swanley. He had been there on that slip road, Decabral had said from the witness box at Noye's trial; he had seen the murder.

And now Alan Decabral popped up once more, this time, however, as the victim. But it was not his testimony in court so much as his appearance which stuck in the mind and which so many instantly recalled when pictures of the man flashed onto the screens and appeared in the newspapers. Who could forget the grossly fat, 20-stone man with the beard and the untidy tangle of greying shoulder-length hair? And wasn't it dreadful for a man who had supported the cause of justice so firmly to end up as he had done?

Kenneth Noye, tucked away in Whitemoor prison, Cambridgeshire, was the obvious suspect. The fact that he was serving a life sentence did not prevent his controlling events outside. A millionaire's powers are not restricted by prison bars. Was this Noye's payback time? But, even though he was interviewed, there was, right from the start, doubt about the gangster's participation in this affair. Quite early in the investigation, a senior police officer said, 'The killer may well be someone else. This murder may well be nothing to do with the Old Bailey trial, but Kenny Noye is the one suspect we have at this time.'

Kenneth Noye was – and, even behind

Alan Decabral, shot in the head.

bars, he still is – a dangerous man. A professional criminal, he had been gaoled for 14 years in 1986 for handling gold from one of the world's biggest gold bullion robberies, the £26 million Brinks-Mat case. And in 1985 he had admitted stabbing John Fordham, an undercover policeman, in the grounds of his West Kingsdown mansion. A jury had on that occasion found he acted in self-defence.

Had Noye, in a spirit of revenge, now killed one of those who had acted as a witness against him? Well, the police gave round-the-clock protection to twelve people who had given evidence at the trial. Danielle Cable, the fiancée of Stephen Cameron, the victim in the road rage incident, had adopted a new identity since the trial. Immediately after the trial, at a few minutes' notice, she was relocated, cutting off for several months all ties with her family, and even today she does not openly meet them. For the rest of her life, it is said, she will hide from possible contract killers.

At the Old Bailey trial in April 2000, Decabral told how he had been at the Swanley interchange of the M20 and the M25. There had been an incident between a Bedford Rascal van driven by 17-year-old Danielle Cable and Noye's dark coloured L-registration Land Rover Discovery. When the cars pulled up at the intersection, Noye and Danielle's fiancé, Stephen Cameron, had had an altercation; words and then blows were exchanged when both men left their vehicles.

In court Decabral gave a detailed account of what next occurred: 'I saw a bright flash and I realized it was a knife because I could see the sun glinting off the blade ... I saw the knife go into his chest. I saw the blood. I'll never forget his face ... I could see him shut the blade with both hands and put it back in his right-hand pocket.' At this point, as Cameron, blood pouring from his chest, staggered in the roadway, Decabral said that Noye strolled past his car, nodding at him as if to say, 'That's sorted him out.' It had. Stephen Cameron was dying. Noye then drove off. Decabral described how he had made a 999 call and had then given chase in his Rolls-Royce but had lost his quarry in heavy traffic. He was, however, able to help the police with an e-fit of the murderer.

It was Decabral's dramatic testimony as much as any other witness's contribution which led to the conviction and life sentence for Kenneth Noye. And now Decabral himself was slain. Was it not reasonable to assume that the long arm of Kenneth Noye had reached out from Whitemoor to a man who had been such a significant witness at his trial?

But why was it, people asked, that Alan Decabral had not been more closely protected by the police? Was the Witness Protection Scheme inadequate? How was it that Decabral had been so let down by the justice system for which he had done such signal service? He had after all been threatened both before and after the trial. In July 2000 the *Sunday Mirror* reported that prior to standing in the witness box Decabral had telephone calls telling him 'to shut up or we will shut you up'. A day or so after that threat, three live bullets were pushed through his letterbox. The message seemed clear. After the trial, and only shortly before his death, he told the *Sunday Mirror*, 'I look over my shoulder every time I go into Sainsbury's.'

Yet the police now claimed that these threats were never reported to them and they revealed that Alan Decabral had not wished to be part of the Witness Protection Scheme. All that he had asked for were police emergency telephone numbers that he could ring if ever he felt himself in danger. And the facts are more complex than at first appeared. Alan Decabral carried a considerable amount of baggage, of which the public knew nothing. People might perhaps have wondered at how such a sloppy looking man could possibly afford to run a Rolls Royce. It doesn't do, we are told, to judge books by their covers, but nevertheless it is difficult sometimes just to suppress the odd query and in Decabral's case it was especially so, in view of the colourful detail which emerged about his life.

The police knew that their important witness had a serious criminal background. He had made a fortune from cocaine and heroin, from large-scale bootlegging of alcohol and tobacco from the Continent, and from providing guns to other active criminals. He was not a small fish in the murky pond in which he swam. He was a provider, a fixer; whatever was wanted, in whatever quantities, he could supply. Notorious and nasty, he had clout.

After Noye's trial, Decabral moved from his home in Lewisham to Pluckley. Perhaps he felt it might be marginally safer. He paid £350,000 cash down for the new house in the village – no need for a mortgage for a high roller like Alan Decabral. At this time he was the owner of several cars, including the Rolls and a Jaguar. In three police raids carried out on this house – one of them only two days before his murder – enormous sums of loose cash were found. Of course, there is no law against keeping loose cash in the house, but in this case? And there were other factors in the seedy, depraved and violent world which Decabral occupied. He was a ladies' man, involved apparently with several women. After the Noye trial, Decabral left his wife, Anne-Marie, and she had much to say publicly, both before and after his death. Hell hath no fury...

The *Sunday Mirror*, slavering over her story, ran an article headed 'My Alan Lied to Jail Noye'. She would stand up in court if they wanted her to, she said. 'Now wife of murdered key witness says: "I'll give evidence for him at appeal"', went the subheading. Her husband, she told the *Mirror*'s readers, had embroidered what he had seen on the slip road in order to stop a police investigation into his drugs and firearms activities. As for the story that he had given chase when Noye drove away from the murder scene, that was just so much invention. Decabral wanted to be away as quickly as possible; he did not wish to hang around for the arrival of the police. He had a consignment of cocaine in the car and was on his way to Lewes to drop it off when the fracas which ended Stephen Cameron's life took place. What if the police had insisted on searching his car? He was better out of it, he had told Anne-Marie, and so he invented the story of the chase.

In addition to her natural anger at having been rejected in favour of another woman, what had further persuaded Anne-Marie to spill the beans as far as her husband was concerned was that at Noye's trial, Decabral had given her address in court and thereafter she had feared reprisals against her and the two children. It was in consequence of this fear that she had written to Noye at Whitemoor prison. Later she met Noye's son, Kevin, who had reassured her that she had nothing to fear from his father.

At the Appeal Court in October 2001, Michael Mansfield, QC, representing Noye, argued that the testimony of such a man as Decabral was worthless and that therefore his client's conviction ought to be overturned. Decabral was a drugs and firearms dealer who had received preferential treatment from the police, Mansfield said. He claimed that after a raid on Decabral's Lewisham home in 1999 the police found 36 grams of cocaine; £160,000, mainly in £50 notes; 56 weapons, including machine guns; and a Mercedes with a concealed compartment for carrying drugs. But, Mansfield informed the court, the investigating officers had neglected to carry out adequate forensic tests on the items found in the house and had chosen not to prosecute Decabral, whose cash and guns, some of them deactivated, were returned to him before the trial. The impression given was that in return for his not being prosecuted, Decabral would not renege on his evidence. 'There's no longer any inevitability that a jury would have convicted, had they known the full picture about Decabral,' Michael Mansfield told the judges.

But the appeal was rejected. 'Putting Mr Decabral's evidence to one side,' said Lord Woolf, the Lord Chief Justice, 'the only conclusion one could come to was that the jury would come to exactly the same verdict.' There had been no excuse for Noye to draw a knife.

However, none of this helps to solve the murder of Alan Decabral. According to some police sources, he had many enemies in the criminal world, and Kenneth Noye was only one of these. In fact there appears to have been a veritable queue of people wishing to be rid of him. Moreover, would Noye, as intelligent as he is ruthless, wish to harm his impending appeal? In fact, the death of Decabral could not have come at a worse time. Such factors contribute to the conclusion that Kenneth Noye was innocent of planning the murder; Decabral's murder at such a sensitive time could have seriously harmed Noye's case.

Decabral, then, had played a major part in the conviction of Noye for the road rage murder. He knew – he must have

Kenneth Noye.

known – the influence wielded by Noye in the underworld. Why did he not retract his evidence? Did he assume that Noye, with his appeal coming up, would simply shrug his shoulders and dismiss the matter from his mind? Or did he think himself safe, even without the cover of the Witness Protection Scheme? Or had the raids on his houses at Lewisham and Pluckley, with all the evidence the police had accumulated about his activities, made it impossible for him to withdraw his evidence?

After the trial, Alan Decabral, always with his mind on business, wanted to be rid of the smothering police presence. How could he conduct drugs deals with the police constantly there? How could he engage in his weapons trade or the money laundering? He would be hindered at every turn. He could not have the police hanging around all the time; it would drive him out of business. When the threats came, he still did not go to the police. He announced to the world through the tabloids that he was being threatened. Perhaps he thought that potential assassins would be dissuaded from trying to kill him if he sought to highlight his position in this way.

Even after he left Lewisham, Decabral did not go into hiding. He was only a matter of 50 miles or so from his old haunts. He made no change of identity and he was an obvious figure in the village in a county favoured by influential criminals. Furthermore, 20-stone men do not easily conceal themselves, especially when they advertise themselves by being banned from the local pub for fighting. He must have felt himself safe.

And what of other enemies? Look at Decabral again: the long, unkempt hair; the arrogant swagger. He was a biker, a former Hell's Angel, thought now to have been a key member of criminal chapters of Hell's Angels and deeply involved in drugs, protection and prostitution. Nowadays some biker gangs fight among themselves for their share in these enterprises. Had Alan Decabral overstepped the mark in his drugs and gun deals with one of these gangs? Had he been punished for double-dealing, selling poor quality drugs, ripping off men who would not stand for being ripped off? Or, as some have implied, had he become too closely involved with the girlfriend of some or other powerful biker baron?

Oddest of all is the coincidence that placed these people, all strangers to each other, one Sunday morning on the slip road at

Swanley. That Sunday morning there was a girl in a van, whose poor driving possibly enraged the man in the Range Rover. It led within minutes to the murder of Stephen Cameron. And in the queue of cars on the same slip road was Alan Decabral in his Rolls Royce. Of course, his death is not necessarily linked to the murder of Stephen Cameron; he might have died in precisely the way he did, had he never even set eyes on Kenneth Noye and his knife glinting in the sun.

IN AN ENGLISH
COUNTRY GARDEN

———————— ✿ ————————

It's not what a milkman expects to find in a neat country garden on a fine Saturday morning in May, the body of a woman. Sprawled on her back across a flower bed, she lay at the foot of a honeysuckle bush. Her bloodied white nightdress was awry, torn at the shoulder, but it was her injuries which were so horrifying, for her head had been savagely battered, and, more than that, she had been shot in the face and the blood had flowed across her cheeks, down her breasts, and formed a pool on the grass. The milkman, David Pilcher, did not linger, for there was nothing that he could do. He called the police. When PC Allen arrived, he was no less horrified than Pilcher had been. He spotted a damaged double-barrelled shotgun, its stock missing, lying on the grass a few feet from where the woman lay. Venturing inside the bungalow, he found a small white dog in a bedroom cupboard. In the scullery he made another discovery: another body, this time a man in pyjamas. He too had been shot in the face.

A double murder in little Aldington? It seemed inconceivable. Who would have wanted to kill in such a brutal fashion such a quiet couple as the Buxtons? They had not been in the village long, only two years or so, and they had seemed so happy and devoted. Roderick Buxton, 35 years old, was such a respectable and hard-working man, well-educated, and employed as a gardener by Miss Gladys de Pomeroy of Pantiles, a large house in extensive grounds. The bungalow in Frith Road went with his job. His wife, Alice, three or four years older than her husband, was Belgian, an attractive, vivacious woman, who worked in a hotel in Hythe as a waitress and chambermaid.

By the afternoon, there were 60 policemen and dogs searching Romney Marsh in case the killer had gone to ground there. In the next two days, whilst there were no arrests, the police were able to pick up other scents. Inevitably, local people were questioned. One story came up that in the previous year a short, dark man had been making enquiries in the neighbourhood about the Buxtons. More immediately there was a suggestion that on the night before the murder a foreign-looking man had been seen in the neighbourhood. He too was short and dark complexioned, and rather suspiciously he had disappeared into a wood when he saw people looking at him. In case this mysterious man was responsible for the murders, ports and airfields were put on heightened alert.

The more the police delved, the more the Buxtons' background unravelled. The major fact was that Alice and Roderick were not married. She was Alice Bateman, who in 1953 had left her husband, Richard, whom she had met when he was serving in Belgium during the war. In 1949, now married, they had gone to live in Evesham, where he set up in business as an agricultural contractor, dealing also in scrap metal and old cars.

It was then that the bachelor, Roderick Buxton, came on the scene. He had a market garden in Evesham and there came a time when he needed lodgings. He moved in with the Batemans and then out with Alice, the two of them setting themselves up in a number of locations until 1959, when they arrived at Aldington. Richard Bateman, heart-broken, searched everywhere for Alice but eventually left for Canada, where he set up as a general dealer. It was said, however, that he had been back to England in 1960. Was it he, the police wondered, who on the night of Friday, 12th May 1961, had committed the Pantiles Bungalow murders? A close lookout was kept on those leaving for Canada by air or sea.

In a short time more emerged: not so much about Roderick, about whom little but good was heard, but the picture of Alice was filling out. There was nothing devastatingly bad, but increasingly the police were to learn that she was an enthusiastic dancer, often going off to dances by herself, sometimes at Folkestone or Hythe or other seaside resorts. She could not always get home after dances and in consequence had to stay with friends. Really? the police wondered. Did her so-called husband always know where she was, who she was staying with? There were suggestions that perhaps he did not. Several men in the area were asked about her.

Detective Chief Superintendent James Jenner of the Kent CID called on Scotland Yard's Murder Squad to assist with the investigation. Help arrived in the person of Detective Chief Superintendent John du Rose, whose skill and speed in solving crimes had given rise to his nickname 'Four-day Johnny'. He was accompanied by Detective Sergeant Roy Habershon. Then along came Francis Camps, the celebrated Home Office pathologist, who assisted the police in formulating a picture of what had occurred at Pantiles Bungalow.

Camps' assessment was that the deaths had occurred shortly before midnight. Some neighbours, admittedly none of them especially close to the bungalow, claimed to have heard shouting at about that time.

The killer was thought to have laid siege to the bungalow for more than half an hour. The emerging picture was that at about eleven o'clock, when the Buxtons (it is more convenient to call Roderick and Alice by this name) were preparing for bed, the murderer called. It was about that time when people said they heard loud voices. Some even thought that they might have heard shots being fired. It seemed that the caller had refused to leave and that the Buxtons had shut the front door on him, hoping that he would calm down and leave them. But the visitor had refused to go. Instead he had fired his shotgun through the scullery window. The couple, in fear for their lives, had flung themselves on the floor, knocking over a table and chairs in their panic. Then more shots were fired from outside.

Roderick had run into the bedroom in an effort to escape or perhaps to try to make his way through a window so that he could surprise the gunman in the garden. But suddenly the muzzle of a shotgun had smashed the window glass. A shot was fired and Roderick was hit in the face. The blood splattered across the walls and floor as the mortally wounded man staggered into the kitchen.

The killer then forced his way into the house and Alice, screaming, made for the back door but not quickly enough, for he struck her several violent blows before she managed to escape into the garden. Again he caught her, this time by the flower beds, by the honeysuckle bush, and with the butt of the shotgun clubbed her with such ferocity that the barrels of the gun were seriously damaged. Then the murderer fired a round into her face. As he ran off, he dropped the damaged part of the gun, which was later found near Alice's body.

The search for the missing part of the shotgun went on. On the

Mrs. Alice Bateman known as Mrs. Buxton.
(Evening Standard, 12 June, 1961)

Saturday afternoon members of the Aldington fire brigade were called from a cricket match and still in their white flannels drained two ponds near the bungalow. Policemen were also detailed to dig up the garden to see if they could find it but nothing was found.

In the house the police came across a suitcase of letters written to Alice, several in affectionate terms. Some were written in Flemish and du Rose asked Interpol for information about young men in Ostend who might have been friends of the murdered woman. Had she a continental lover? Was this a crime of passion? Then, under the bed, police found a torn-up letter along with its registered envelope. The letter had been posted to Alice in Belgium on May 8th and then redirected to her home address, where it had arrived on the morning of May 12th. Roderick Buxton had signed for its delivery. Written in English, its terms suggested that there was some fairly intimate association between Alice and the writer of the letter. 'I still think of you because I love you,' he had written. It concluded: 'Bye bye, Hendryk, kiss you,' with a row of kisses.

Hendryk? Hendryk Niemasz, a 40-year-old Pole, who had settled in England after the war, lived with his wife and two children on a smallholding in Laws Lane, Mersham, not half a mile away from Pantiles Bungalow. Niemasz at the time of the murder was working away from home on building sites, lodging during the week in Gillingham. He and Alice, the police learned, had been seen together on several occasions. Of course, they had been seen, Niemasz said when questioned; they were good friends. For the past year he and his wife Grypa had been friendly with the Buxtons. They often went out together. On the night of May 12th, Niemasz told the police, he had motored home from Gillingham for the weekend and at the time of the murder was in bed. His wife confirmed this.

After the visit by the police, Niemasz spoke to the press, although the newspaper report does not hint at his fumbling with the English language, which he had not mastered. 'The police examined my shoes and clothes and wanted to know when I last saw the Buxtons,' Niemasz said. 'I know that in the village they say she has been in my car a lot. But there was nothing in that. I just used to give her lifts to work sometimes because she was a friend. She liked a gay life, going to dances. She used to ask my wife to go but she never would. But I have seen her meet many men.'

Ah yes, he had seen her meet many men. Niemasz's comment was not the first of that kind. The police were still questioning other men in Folkestone and Hythe, but they persisted in their questions to Niemasz. Did he have some kind of relationship with her, he was asked. 'Just friends,' he replied. 'I have missus! I no want Alice or other woman!' he said. But yes, he had written to her recently, only a few days ago. She was in Belgium and he had written to ask when she was due to arrive in Dover so that they could meet her. And the kisses? 'Alice put kisses. I put kisses. Everyone put kisses,' he explained.

For two or three days more Niemasz was in the clear, but then detectives made their breakthrough. They returned to search Niemasz's house and garden. In a tumbledown shed they found the broken stock of a double-barrelled shotgun and three live cartridges, hidden under the hay used for pigs' bedding. It belonged to a shotgun of the type used in the murder. It was examined and it matched exactly the part of the gun found in the Buxtons' garden. The two parts of the shotgun, spotted and smeared with human blood, were sent to the forensic laboratories at Scotland Yard.

The police now felt able to arrest their prime suspect. Within four days, Detective Superintendent John du Rose must have reflected with some satisfaction. Early on Wednesday, Hendryk Niemasz was picked up on the Cuxham building site where he was working as a labourer and taken to Rochester for questioning. From there he was taken to Ashford police station. From this time until his trial, the Pole was desperately confused, continually changing his story, inventing new lines for himself.

In the magistrates' court and later at his four-day trial in July at the Sussex Assizes in Lewes, Niemasz was alleged to have told the police, 'I no kill her. I pay man £60 to kill Alice. I not angry with Roderick.' He had gone on to say, 'Alice very wicked woman.' She had told him, 'You come away with me. I like change of husbands.'

'I love my children,' Niemasz claimed he had told her. 'I have missus. I not want to go with you.' But this wicked woman would not leave him alone. 'Alice has been after me,' Niemasz said. 'My missus no like it. She said, "You got to keep away."'

Alice had sent him a letter, he said, urging him to go away with her. 'I show letter to man in pub,' Niemasz had told the police. And the man had listened sympathetically. 'Me tell him she wicked woman and he say he help me. He kill Alice for £100. I say I have only £60. He say all right. I gave man £60. I take him in motor and show him where Alice live. He had gun in sack. Me go home to missus. Next morning I met man in other place. Me no want Roderick killed. Only want Alice killed. She bad woman.'

Credible? A man in a pub, a total stranger called George, says he is willing to help out a fellow drinker's predicament? Well, perhaps no less credible than the other part of the story. 'I was in Army,' Niemasz said in a statement to the police. 'I not kill anybody but this time I was fright for my wife and my family.' He had tried to reject Alice, he said. 'I say I would not leave my wife. I love my wife and children. She showed me a little gun. She said, "Get rid of your wife. Your wife is finished. I be your wife."' Later he claimed that Alice had said to him: 'I kill Roderick. You have gun. Finish wife and children.'

PC Dennis Large, escorting Niemasz to Seabrook Court, reported that the accused man had turned to him. 'What they do to me?' he had asked. 'I kill Alice. I no kill Roderick. I no angry with him.' The constable warned Niemasz. There was no need to tell him anything, he told the evidently distressed man. But that did not stop the confession. 'I kill because she would kill wife and two children,' Niemasz insisted. 'He say I kill Alice but other man with me he kill him. I pay £60.' This was exactly what he said to the magistrates later that morning. 'Other man help me.

He shoot gun at someone in window. Then she jumped out kitchen door and we kill her.'

Despite a series of conflicting statements, Niemasz's most consistent version has the hired killer shooting Roderick.

What had led up to this disastrous affair has never been absolutely clear. The impression Niemasz tried to convey was that the love affair with Alice suddenly became too intense, so out of hand, with her asking him to run away with her after murdering his family. He related that only a day or so before her death she had said to him: 'One day I think we be together. I escape with you some place.' It had all proved too much for him, he claimed, with the insistence that he murder his family. But the most likely motive is that he murdered Alice because she wished to end their affair. He had loved her deeply when the letter was sent to her on May 8th. By May 12th, some other emotion had governed his actions.

A remarkable feature of this case is that Niemasz's 14-year-old son, Johnny, was called to give evidence in camera. The prosecution alleged that he had written the letter found under the Buxtons' bed, one of the links in the chain of evidence against Niemasz. However, the boy had written it at his father's dictation, as Niemasz, at least in English, was illiterate. The defence in the magistrates' court was strongly opposed to Johnny Niemasz being placed in this difficult position. Mr Coley, defending, said, 'in no case of this nature in similar circumstances has a child ever been called to give evidence against his own father. If his evidence is admitted and if the accused should be found guilty he has got to live for the rest of his life with the knowledge that he might have given some evidence which may have been a factor in condemning the father. He is not English and I do not know how well he understands our ways and customs or indeed how well he speaks English.' It was, Mr Coley said, not only unfair to the boy but to all the family. 'One can well imagine,' counsel continued, 'what their attitude might be in the future if he is allowed to give evidence against his father.' There was a matter here of great principle not only on the part of the defendant but as regards children's rights in general.

What is not known is whether Roderick Buxton had read the letter sent to his wife. After signing for it, had he opened it and later confronted Alice, accusing her of having an affair with Niemasz? Did he then demand that she end the affair?

The next crucial phase was in the evening. Roderick was last seen tending the flower beds at Pantiles House at 7.15. At about ten o'clock, Hendryk Niemasz's cream Hillman Husky was seen outside Pantiles Bungalow. He had left his lodgings in St George's Road in Gillingham an hour or so earlier. Had there been an altercation when he called at the bungalow? Why did he go there at that time of night? Was Niemasz distraught on learning that Alice now wished to discontinue their affair? Had Roderick challenged him about the letter which had arrived earlier that day? Whatever the case, Niemasz had then driven home, found his shotgun and then, according to his wife after she realised that she could no longer maintain his alibi, he had left the house again on his cycle. He is a spurned lover who slaughters Alice in an uncontrollable rage. His hurt is so deep and he cannot forgive her for letting him down so. Roderick is shot simply because he is there.

In the days and weeks to come Niemasz could not forgive her. She was the author of all his ills. She was, he would say, a wicked woman who urged him to murder his wife. Surely, he maintained, the system of justice would recognise what she had put him through, how her wicked actions had made him do what he did. They surely could not hang him for that. Of course, he acknowledges that there is no reprieve from Roderick's murder. There is no excuse

Hendryk Niemasz. (Daily Telegraph and Morning Post, 13 June, 1961)

for that. But he did not do it. George did that, he tells police, magistrates, judge and jury.

But the letter and the concealed shotgun bearing Alice's blood and Niemasz's fingerprints tell too heavily against him, and Grypa finds it impossible to maintain his alibi in view of the evidence against her husband. The mysterious George, never found, who was willing to fix a stranger's troubles for £60, is too far-fetched for the jury to swallow. After 75 minutes the jury returned a verdict of guilty. Niemasz was sentenced to hang for the murder of Roderick Buxton and also sentenced to life imprisonment for the non-capital murder of Alice.

This was undoubtedly a crime of passion, committed by a man desperate for the love of a woman he was losing, but that could not save him, not in England. When he heard the translator tell him the verdict he said he did not understand why he was accused. He told the translator to say to the judge that he was innocent. 'I didn't do it. I didn't do it,' he insisted. He stood by his story that he did not kill Roderick. As he was finally led from the dock, he shook his head and said, as he disappeared down the steps, 'No understand, no understand.' But no part of Hendryk Niemasz's story, none of his assertions of innocence, could prevent him from being, on 8th September 1961, the last man to hang at Wandsworth prison.

A PRESENCE AT
DENE MANOR

———————❊———————

Dene Manor at Meopham is haunted – unsurprisingly so, for it is a medieval building, parts of it dating back to the 15th century, and its lands are mentioned in the Domesday Book. Old places like this have seen enacted enough dramatic events and have watched the traumas of too many of their various occupants not to carry the ripples of the past into the present. Dene Manor has been home to people of power and influence, men and women at the centre of national events. An Archbishop of Canterbury was born here, and one of its former owners went off to the crusades with Richard the Lionheart. At times in the last six or seven hundred years or so there will have been disagreements here, sadnesses, anger, even violence, among people accustomed to having their own way. There has been at least one suicide and there is talk of the murder of a servant girl. Perhaps it is she who disturbs the atmosphere today, her muffled footfalls heard throughout the house, but mainly on the stairway from the main dining room to the upper floor. Perhaps it is her tap-tap-tapping that is so often heard; perhaps she is responsible for the doors which seem to open of their own volition, especially the wine cellar door, which seems to be the focus of the abnormal manifestations. Is it her restless spirit, that shaft of cold air from an unknown origin, that chills the lower floor?

The Dene Manor disturbances are not Meopham's sole acquaintance with the supernatural. Tales are told of the ghost of a miller who hanged himself in a barn, and there is, so it is said, a headless monk who walks near the church, though little else is known of him, neither his name nor his history. Better known is the shade of Mlle. Pinard who followed her lover from France, whom she first met in the wars against Napoleon. Loyal and loving, she came to his home in Meopham only to discover he had a wife. Wretched and abandoned, she hanged herself in her fine orange silk gown, and ever since she has wandered disconsolately along Steeles Lane, near the green.

But these were not the ghosts that attracted Harry Price, who in 1936 arranged to broadcast via BBC radio from Dene Manor, to let the public listen in to what was to be a scientifically respectable investigation into the supernatural. At the time Price was the country's pre-eminent investigator into the paranormal. Self-trained, self-financed, independent and enterprising, he had spent a lifetime investigating all manner of abnormal occurrences. He had dealt with poltergeists and with scores of ghost-ridden buildings, among them Borley Rectory, allegedly Britain's most haunted house. He had been involved in the investigation into 'the talking mongoose'; he had studied the claims of various mediums and clairvoyants; he had looked into telepathy, fire-walking and various tricks of an esoteric nature, such as the Indian rope trick. Many he had found to be fraudulent; others, he admitted, could not be accounted for by normal means and were beyond his powers to explain.

In many instances, Price knew the causes of alleged hauntings could be traced to mischievous boys, rats, wind, or shrinking wood. Thus, when he came to Dene Manor on 10th March 1936 in his capacity as Honorary Secretary of the London University Council for Psychical Investigation, he imposed rigid scientific controls on the investigation.

Price was accompanied by the trusted and solidly reliable BBC announcer Freddie Grisewood, whose task it was to comment on the preparations being made to trace the ghost. With them came the philosopher, Professor C E M Joad of Birkbeck College, future stalwart of the BBC's *Brains Trust*. The presence of Grisewood and Joad was to add a certain gravitas to an occasion that some at the BBC were dubious about. Perhaps they felt that the Corporation was dumbing down.

The plan was that the broadcast should be in two parts. For 20 minutes after eight o'clock Grisewood and Price would set the scene, describing to listeners exactly what preparations Price had made in the course of the day, the various methods – visual, aural or thermal – by which he hoped to record any abnormal happenings. Then, from 11.45 pm until midnight, listeners would be able to hear, with any luck, the muffled footsteps, the creaking doors and the tap-tap-taps, all of which seemed to be regularly heard by the house's occupants.

Four microphones were placed strategically to catch the slightest sound. One was put in a walnut tree in the garden; another was in the attic, in the dust and cobwebs of the beams, ties and buttresses; a third was placed on the dining room table, and the fourth was at the focal point of the disturbances, down in the wine cellar. Who knew where the ghost might manifest itself? Electric contacts were attached to the wine cellar door, which was said to open frequently without any assistance. In the event of the door opening, the contacts would set off a red indicator light and so warn the investigators of the presence of a ghost. A camera was focused on the cellar door to record any unassisted movement. In the cellar there was also a thermograph to record any changes in temperature. It is common for the temperature to fall in the presence of paranormal disturbances.

The floor of the cellar and the passageway leading to the hall were sprinkled with finely powdered starch. Any fingerprints were removed from all the doors and windows in the house and then powdered graphite was sprinkled over in readiness, should any ghostly fingerprints appear in the course of the evening's investigation. Lead seals provided by the Post Office were put on the doors and windows for the duration of the broadcast.

Price arranged to keep a log of all that happened during the three and half hours between the two broadcasts. In this time he and his companions made regular visits to the attic and to the cellar, where at intervals they sat on wine casks waiting for something dramatic to happen. At one point in the evening the dining room microphone picked up the sound of water trickling. The three men made their way upstairs to the attic. Sure enough water was trickling into the cistern high up in the roof, but it was no demonstration of ghostly tricks; down in the kitchen the cook had turned the tap on.

Later again Price heard the sound of footsteps in the cellar. But after investigating he concluded that the microphone had picked up the footsteps of one of the investigators walking about on the flagstones of the dining room. Although the dining room was not over the cellar, the joists which supported the room were connected in some way with the cellar roof and these served as conduits for the sounds.

Shortly after ten o'clock, Price went down to the cellar and examined the thermograph which had been installed there. He

A thermograph is installed in the cellar of Dene Manor. (The Listener)

found that from 8 until 8.55 pm the temperature of the cellar was slightly below 47 degrees Fahrenheit. Then, by 9.26 pm, the temperature had gradually fallen by .25 degrees. By 9.44 pm the temperature had risen again by one degree, finally settling at a steady 47.75 degrees.

The thermograph chart was attached to a drum which made a complete revolution every three hours. Price had installed the first drum at eight o'clock, and so it was due to be changed at 11 o'clock. It was then, when changing the drum, that he noticed that curious variations in temperature had occurred in the previous 25 minutes. From 9.44 pm until 10.35 pm the temperature in the cellar did not vary. But then, the graph showed a sudden rise of more than half a degree in three minutes. There was a sudden fall of nearly one degree in three minutes. Then came a steady fall of one degree during the next 13 minutes. After that there was a gradual rise of nearly 1.5 degrees in ten minutes; then, at eleven o'clock, the pen finally ran off the chart.

If these changes of temperature were not particularly impressive, they were interesting because of the suddenness of their variations. The graph representing the temperature during the three hours immediately preceding the first broadcast at eight o'clock showed an almost straight line across the chart. But between 10 and 11 pm the line was by no means straight. But the most curious feature of the variations was that the temperature rose. Temperature falls are common in haunted locations, but Price could think of nothing which would have caused the temperature of the cellar to rise. Had it, the investigators wondered, anything to do with the stoking of the log fire in the dining room? Was that the cause of the temperature variations? But Price was convinced that nothing of the sort could have happened because there was no connection between the two rooms, which were far apart. In any case the fire had been burning in the dining room all day, during which period the temperature in the cellar had remained practically constant.

In the second stage of the broadcast, from 11.45 pm till midnight, Price and Grisewood told listeners that all of the seals on the doors and windows were intact. The powder scattered on the floor and stairs leading to the haunted door was undisturbed, registering only the footprints of Price and his colleagues. There were no mystery fingerprints at all on any of the windows.

It was generally felt that the experiment had failed. The editorial in *The Sunday Times*, describing the experiment as a 'fiasco', reported quite smugly that the haunted house had refused to make an exhibition of itself. 'So universally was the experiment expected to fail that few appear to have examined the awful possibilities of success,' the editor smirked. 'It would have been even more serious if the ghost had been in conversational mood,' he continued. 'Like His Majesty the King, and like nobody else, he had been invited to the microphone without previously submitting his manuscript for censorship and approval. The BBC in fact were taking a grave risk, and it is fortunate indeed that the ghost's sense of responsibility was stronger than theirs.'

Certainly there had been insufficient activity to convince listeners that the broadcast was worth sitting up for. Where were the sounds of footsteps?

Why had there been no tampering with the door seals? Were there not even the slightest smudges on the powdered floorboards? It was all very disappointing. Was there nothing creepy to report,

The haunted door. (The Listener)

nothing to send listeners looking over their shoulders as they went off to their beds? That the thermograph should record modest rises and sudden falls in temperature was not enough to cause the hair to bristle on the back of the neck.

Nevertheless, the temperature did rise and it did fall and the question remains: did these variations in temperature occur because of a presence in the wine cellar? Had some restless resident spirit of Dene Manor come there? Was a ghost there for some of the time?

The Dene Manor experiment might be accounted a farce and a failure by some, but others will maintain the view that experiments conducted scientifically do sometimes fail – but that that alone does not disprove their value.

AN OFF-SHORE
MURDER

———————— ❁ ————————

Even in the glitzy land of bodies of sculpted golden bronze, of regular, whiter-than-white teeth, and of eternal youth, Graham Miller was admired. He was a positive head-turner whose film-star looks were topped up with a winning personality. Charming and well-mannered, a sharp dresser and a BMW-driver, Graham seemed to have everything.

Breezy and confident, a 28-year-old fitness trainer in a San Fernando Valley health club, Graham had hopes of becoming a film stuntman and was sure that in a year or two he would make it in Hollywood. But his confidence must have taken a tumble the day he was arrested at the club under his real name, Neville van der Merwe. After seven years he had finally been run down.

Three years earlier a judge in South Africa had declared in Van der Merwe's absence that when found he must go before the British courts. Kent police, eventually learning that he was in the USA, contacted the US Immigration Service, whose computers traced him to California. Then came Van der Merwe's arrest and deportation to the UK. In 1999 he appeared at the Old Bailey, charged with the abduction and murder of Simon Law.

Rewind to 1991. It's England, deep in downland Kent, in Elmsted, a quiet, small, scattered community, and the quiet country lane which leads to Beech Tree Farm, Simon Law's beautiful 17th-century farmhouse. At 35-years-old, Law is a high-powered accountant who works from home; he is an expert in working out how best to place money so that it cannot be greedily grasped by the taxman. The man in the street cannot afford the Oxford mathematics graduate's skills. But big business can.

And then one day Simon Law disappears, and up to the time of writing this account he has not been seen.

But stay in the same Elmsted lane, where Joan Risby is a keen

Neighbourhood Watch representative. She takes her role seriously and on the afternoon of Wednesday, 17th April, she notices a red car in the lane. It passes her house and goes on, she assumes, to Beech Tree Farm. It is not Simon's car – he has a Range Rover – and it isn't his girlfriend's car, and in any case she usually comes down just at weekends. Not many strange cars pass down the lane, and so Joan records the registration – E377BWV – in her notebook. There are two men in the car, which turns at the end of the lane. Simon is not at home. His car is not in the drive.

And now it's the morning of the next day, Thursday, 18th April, and Joan Risby spots the same red car parked for a while near her house. Then several hours later, at 5.30 pm, it's back. It's the same car, Joan is certain, and the same men too. She checks the registration number but that is not the same as yesterday. She writes it down – E635DGX. Perhaps it's a different car but the same model; that may be the explanation. Again the car turns and leaves. Simon Law is away from home again.

The car is back the following afternoon, Friday, and again Joan notes the time and registration number.

On Tuesday, 23rd April, at 7.30 in the morning, the car is in the lane yet again. Minutes later it is in the gravel yard in front of Simon Law's house. His Range Rover is there. At last the visitors have found him at home. It's odd that they just turned up on the off-chance of finding him in. Why not make an appointment? Then, 20 minutes later, Joan hears a car driving past her house. She doesn't see it. Perhaps it's the red car; she can't be sure.

Law's girlfriend, Tarn Phillips, worked for Deloittes in London as an accountant, but on the Monday and throughout Tuesday she had become increasingly anxious. Simon always rang on Mondays. But on Monday, 22nd April, he did not. She telephoned him several times on the Tuesday and received no reply. There must be some explanation, she told herself. When he came up to her South London flat for lunch, as he always did on Wednesdays, doubtless he would explain exactly what had happened. It would be some urgent matter which had taken him away from home but which had given him no time to contact her. But Simon did not turn up for lunch.

Now seriously worried, Tarn telephoned Ann Nichols, one of Simon's neighbours, who had keys to Beech Tree Farm. Would she call over at the house to see if Simon was all right, she asked. Within minutes Ann Nichols telephoned back. The house was

Neville van der Merwe.

open, she said, but Simon was not there.

At once Tarn motored down to Beech Tree Farm. She found the Range Rover in the driveway. As Ann Nichols had told her, the front door was open. On the doorstep there were two pints of milk. Inside, the radio was playing. There was a half-used bottle

Simon Law and Tarn Phillips.

of milk on the kitchen table. Simon's bed had been slept in but it was not made up. On his bedside table were his keys and some loose change. His passport was in the drawer. There was water in the bath, and there were clothes on the bathroom floor. Simon's grey bathrobe, which usually hung behind the bedroom door, was missing. There was no sign of a struggle but Tarn was of the view that Simon had been kidnapped. There would be a call for a ransom, she was sure. She telephoned the police.

Police were soon searching the house and the area. A police helicopter guided them as they looked in fields and copses. Detective Chief Inspector George Rogers of Kent CID headed the investigation and began by interviewing neighbours. Joan Risby presented her invaluable notebook. Sonia Shepherd, who lived in a nearby cottage, told the police how one morning during the previous week a stranger had asked the way to Beech Tree Farm. She said that he had a strong accent – perhaps it was Irish – and she noticed another man waiting in a fairly new Vauxhall.

Ann Nichols' husband, James, recalled conversations with Simon Law. Law had spoken about a serious dispute with David Jenkins, a South African businessman, the owner of South Africa's largest container-leasing operation, Multistar Containers Transport. For some years Law had managed Jenkins' extensive off-shore financial affairs but had become increasingly uncomfortable about their shady nature. Recently there had been a serious falling-out between the men. Only weeks earlier, Law had told Nichols that matters were still not resolved. 'I wouldn't be surprised if he didn't send over a couple of blokes to sort me out,' Law had said. At the time James Nichols perhaps had put down the remark to a half-jocular exaggeration, but now it was certainly something he felt the police ought to know about.

Police were now seeking the red Vauxhall. On Saturday, 20th April, they received reports that the licence plates had been stolen some days earlier from a Vauxhall Cavalier left in a parking lot in Ashford. The stolen number plates – E635DGX – tallied with the car seen in the lane by Joan Risby on the Thursday. Meanwhile the police had checked the national computer base for details of ownership of the car which Mrs Risby had seen for the first time on the Wednesday. The car registered E377BWV belonged to Chris Pollard, who lived in London. Within an hour of receiving this information police were at Pollard's house. And what a tale he had to tell.

Pollard had a cousin, Graham Moore, who had recently had a couple of young friends from South Africa staying with his parents at their house in Farnham in Surrey. They had not visited the country before and in their short stay they wanted to see as much of England as possible. When Graham Moore mentioned this to Pollard, although he did not know the South Africans, he had agreed to lend them his red Vauxhall Astra. The car was borrowed for the first time on April 17th, when the young men said they wanted to go to Ashford. Chief Inspector Rogers noted that Ashford, where the licence plates were stolen, was on the direct route to Elmsted for someone driving from Surrey. On their return the men said that they had gone on from Ashford to Dover where the white cliffs were 'a disappointment'. The car was used on April 18th and 19th too. On April 22nd the men borrowed the car again, saying that they wished to visit a friend. They returned the car on the evening of April 23rd. The following day, their visit over, the young men returned to South Africa.

Moore's Astra was now taken away for forensic examination. It was perfectly clean. The men had vacuumed and washed it on the night they returned it, prior to flying home the next day. The only clue was a single blood stain on the rubber rim of the boot. This was sent for analysis. DNA profiling analysis said it was 1.5 million times more likely that the blood originated from a child of Isaac and Nancy Law than from a person taken at random from the general population.

Chief Inspector Rogers went to Farnham to question Graham Moore further about his two friends. In 1982, Moore explained, he was employed as an engineer in South Africa. One friend he made was Glenn Chait. In 1985 Moore returned to England and more or less lost all contact with his South African friends. Then, quite out of the blue, in late March or early April 1991, he received an unexpected telephone call from Chait. He said that he was planning to visit England shortly to check on the authenticity of a Talbot car. As he did not know the country, he wondered if Moore could spare time to help him. Of course he could, Moore had told his old friend.

On Sunday, 13th April, 39-year-old Chait landed at Heathrow. With him was another South African, 20-year-old Neville van der Merwe. Moore met them and offered them accommodation in his parents' home in Farnham during their stay. A day or two later, Moore's cousin, Chris Pollard, offered to lend them his car.

Moore, now horrified that the two South Africans might be involved in the abduction and possible murder of Simon Law, was anxious to co-operate with the police. On one occasion, he recalled, he was returning from a bar with drinks and Chait and Van der Merwe were speaking in Afrikaans. During his stay in South Africa, Moore had picked up enough of the language to recognise some words. He understood, from the slight snatch of conversation that he heard, that the men were talking about a percentage and wondering how much they were going to make out of 'the deal'. He heard the figure 82,000 mentioned, but he did not know if this referred to rands or pounds. At that point the conversation ended. At the time it had not made much impression. 'The deal', he had imagined, related to the Talbot car.

Then Moore's father recalled that when his guests came back from one of their overnight trips – he thought it was their last, on April 23rd – they had washed the red Vauxhall and vacuumed its interior. Chait's boots, he remembered, had been covered in mud.

The police in Britain and in South Africa were seriously wondering now if David Jenkins, the South African container tycoon, had had anything to do with the disappearance of Simon Law. Had he sent two hit men to the UK with the express purpose of ridding himself of a man who now posed a danger to him? Chait and Van der Merwe, those grateful guests of the Moores, had with such thoughtfulness washed the car so kindly lent to them by Chris Pollard. Could these friends of Graham Moore really be hit men? George Rogers certainly intended to ask them. Chait seemed interesting; he was a former policeman and was now an occasional 'debt enforcer'.

Meanwhile, Charles Tarry, Law's former business partner, produced further background material about the dispute between Law and Jenkins, which began in 1988. In recent months, he said, it had become very serious. The South African courts had decided that Jenkins must pay Law a substantial sum in outstanding fees by April 1991. Jenkins said that Law had ripped him off. At the same time, the South African Reserve Bank was investigating Jenkins' offshore business dealings. They suspected him of a so-called 'round tripping' currency fraud involving cargo containers. This was an especially difficult problem for Jenkins. The investors in his complicated investment scheme were rich and influential South Africans who had poured millions into the venture. And Jenkins, it was said, knew that Law had enough information to send him to prison and lose his investors their money.

In May 1990, after the two men failed to resolve their differences when they met in London, Law left an angry card for Jenkins at the Cavalry and Guards Club. It read: 'I will see you in Hell for this.' In October 1990 Jenkins and Law met again but, according to Charles Tarry, Jenkins' business methods were not traditional. 'He (Jenkins) wanted to use a tyre lever on Simon Law in order to force us to obey his wishes,' Tarry said. When Tarry and Law met Jenkins the following month, again in London, Tarry described how they 'took two other men with us – in part, to boost our number, because we were genuinely concerned about the possibility of force being used'.

In January 1991 Jenkins threatened to pursue Law and Tarry through the courts 'for the rest of their lives' if they did not carry out his wishes. Jenkins insisted that Law sign documents obliging him to keep secret all details of their past dealings. Anxious about

THE CAVALRY AND GUARDS CLUB

TELEPHONE MESSAGE

Message for: *Mr Q Jenkins* .... Room No ....

From: ....

Message: ....

I will see you in Hell for

this.

Simon

Message Received: Verbally — By Telephone — By Messenger

Message taken by ....*Maud*................................

at ....*14.39*............ a.m./p.m. on ....*14/5*.......... 199......

The Cavalry and Guards Club   Telegraphic Address:
127 Piccadilly, London   Mameluke, London, W.1.
W1V 0PX   Telephone: 071-499 1261 (5 lines)
                                     Fax: 071-495 5956

possible criminal and professional implications, Law refused to sign. At a final meeting in April 1991, Law again refused to sign the secrecy document. Soon after – and of course, there is no proof that the events are related – Glenn Chait and Neville van der Merwe arrived in the UK.

Later the authorities in South Africa and the UK could find no direct proof to proceed against Jenkins as far as the abduction and possible murder of Law were concerned. Nevertheless, Chief Inspector Rogers, who visited South Africa on three occasions, believed that Law had been murdered at his home and his body buried deep in a forest near Elmsted. The search for Chait and Van der Merwe continued but they had gone to ground.

In 1996 Glenn Chait was finally arrested in Johannesburg and the court ordered his extradition to the UK. Days later, he was found hanged in his cell. After a perfunctory inquest, during which no witnesses were called, the magistrate ruled the cause 'or likely cause' of death to be consistent with hanging and brought in a verdict of suicide. One is reminded of Van der Merwe's question to his father when they met shortly after his flight to America. 'Is Glenn Chait still alive?' he asked.

In the meantime, Tarn Phillips continued her struggle to get to the root of the matter. She sent letters to leading figures in South Africa, accusing Jenkins of massive fraud and of having a hand in Simon Law's disappearance. She wrote to the Attorney General expressing her delight that Jenkins had been arrested, but within twelve months all charges were withdrawn. The Reserve Bank later closed down its investigation into Jenkins' affairs.

Neville van der Merwe was deported from the USA in 1998 and in 1999 faced two trials in London. At the first trial the jury failed to reach a verdict. He was acquitted at the second trial. One witness alleged that Van der Merwe had told him that an attempt to frighten Law had got out of hand and that he was beaten to death at Beech Tree Farm but the accused man's assertion that he was in London at the time Law disappeared proved too powerful an alibi.

As far as the law is concerned, the disappearance of Simon Law remains a mystery.

A NEARLY PERFECT MURDER

❁

On Sunday, 5th January 1985 at one o'clock in the morning – the coldest hour of the bitterest night of the winter, a night of bone-aching cold – a stealthy figure, a man, pushes aside the white-rimed branches of the bushes, moving with some caution across the brittle, frosted grass. The beam of his torch lights on clumps of undergrowth, on the trunks of trees, on the pond. He is patient in his task, watching, searching, waiting. And now he pauses, thinking he hears something: a groaning sound. He waits, not moving. He hears the sound again: a wheezing, an animal perhaps, an injured fox. His torch scans the area and there in front of him he sees a woman's legs. Again she moans. He hesitates; he doesn't want to get too mixed up in this. Probably she's drunk. He hasn't time for that. But it is a cold night – too cold for anyone. She could freeze to death on a night such as this. Perhaps he ought to look.

It was a chance in hundreds that Dr Keith Corbett should be there on this particular night. If it had not been for Bromley Council's wanting more evidence about the number of toads crossing Fishponds Road at Keston, he would not have been there. An ecologist, specialising in reptiles and amphibians, he was inspecting the area known as Caesar's Bank, where toads hibernated, though admittedly usually later in the year. If he was to save the lives of toads crossing the road he needed to persuade the council to close the road temporarily during the mating season, and he needed the facts, even if it meant night work in the very depths of winter.

Now, Dr Corbett braced himself to look more closely at the woman lying there in the beam of his torch. She was clothed flimsily, wearing a blouse and dress, but, on this freezing night, she had no overcoat. Tentatively Corbett reached out, touched her. His fingers came away, wet and sticky. 'I thought she'd been sick,' he said later. 'Then I saw the wound with my torch. There was blood everywhere. It was a horrific sight.' He is a scientist. He notices things. Her breathing, for instance, is deep and regular, as if she has been drugged, and there's a ghastly wound to her throat. As a biologist used to dissection, Corbett notes 'a neat dissection'.

Corbett managed to find help and the woman, deeply unconscious but still clinging on to life, was taken to the intensive care unit at Bromley Hospital, where doctors assessed the wound, the savage five-inch gash. Her vocal chords and windpipe had been slashed through, but mercifully no major artery in the neck had been severed. She had lost four, perhaps five pints of blood. The bleeding, fortunately for the victim, had been slowed to a mere trickle by the sub-zero temperature.

The identification of the woman was not difficult. Several hours earlier she had been reported missing by her deeply distressed husband. It had been a special day for Dr John Baksh and his wife Madhu, a partner in his practice, the doctor explained to the police. Earlier, anticipating their wedding anniversary, they had bought diamonds. At home they had opened a celebratory bottle of champagne, and then, while he had had to go out, Madhu had disappeared. When his BMW with its personalised plates – JB 70 – was later found abandoned in Bromley, it seemed that she had been abducted, and her kidnappers, after attempting to slit her throat, had heartlessly abandoned her.

At first 43-year-old Dr Madhu Baksh in her comatose state could not help with any enquiries. Even when she did recover consciousness, she was unable to speak. Attempts to get her to write answers to police questions failed, for she was too weak to hold a pencil. Slowly, however, she gathered strength, her husband supporting her with regular visits, bringing her flowers and magazines. Although he spent time at her bedside, talking to her, she remained generally lacklustre, so severe were her injuries. Then came the first faint attempts at speech.

At first it was believed that Madhu had been attacked by someone desperate for drugs. Nurses thought they heard her murmur 'Methadone' and 'Omnopon' and 'morphine'. This was mentioned to the police, who now wondered if, as a professional partner of her husband, with surgeries in Mottingham and Chislehurst, she had been specifically targeted by a drugs gang.

But it was Dr Keith Corbett, that midnight toad-tracker, who caused the police to think again about Madhu Baksh's horrifying injuries. On the night when he found her, Corbett had been impressed by the elegance of the wound in her throat. There was a quality of precision and delicacy about the injury. It was as if whoever had done this to Madhu was accustomed to making surgical incisions.

Then came along another member of the public to voice his unease about the attempted murder at Keston Ponds. Barry Willmott, a local restaurateur, had heard talk about the 'dreadful incident' up the road but until he saw a picture of Madhu and her husband in the *Kentish Times* he thought little about it. There was an account of the attack on Madhu and, alongside it, a wedding photograph of her and her husband. And Barry Willmott's memory was jogged. He knew the man's face, remembered him, recalled seeing him two years earlier, in 1983. It was New Year's Day and the Willmotts were on holiday in Mojacar in Spain, when a doctor, an Indian, had walked down from his villa and into a bar and had announced, 'My wife is dead.' It had been so matter of fact, so cold, so emotionless, that statement. Willmott had never forgotten the man standing there, making his announcement in so casual a manner. He did not know his name; he didn't realise that he had a medical practice so near to his own restaurant in Kent. In fact, he had never given the matter much thought, not for three years, and then he saw the photograph in the paper. It was him, the man in the Spanish bar. Barry Willmot knew it and he at once contacted the police. Sceptical? Of course they were, but this call and the observations of Keith Corbett opened the door to the whole investigation. Dr John Madhu's intricate tale began to fall apart.

Then came a further breakthrough. On one of the doctor's visits, the policewoman in the room with Madhu heard him ask her if she remembered the two masked men who had dragged her out of the car. But Madhu had simply glared at him and pointed at her throat. When he had left the room Madhu reached for the chalk board and wrote her astounding message. 'My husband is a killer. Tell the judges he killed his first wife.'

When detectives came to interview her again, she mouthed the word *morphine*. Detective Superintendent Norman Stockford, in charge of the case, asked for the tiny blood sample taken from Madhu when she was first admitted to intensive care to be tested.

John and Madhu Bakskh.

The report did not perhaps surprise Stockford. She had been injected with a massive dose of morphine.

Madhu, now recovering, was able to provide a remarkable tale. Her husband, she said, on his visits to hospital had made desperate pleas to her to save him from gaol. He told her to tell police that two masked men had abducted her. And there was more, she told detectives: Baksh had murdered his first wife, Ruby, and he had confessed the murder to her. And, Madhu added, she was here in hospital because he had drugged her, cut her throat, driven her to the woods and left her there to die.

Detective Superintendent Stockford and a Home Office pathologist, Dr Iain West, now went to Spain. With permission from the Spanish authorities, they exhumed Ruby's body from the cemetery at Mojacar. The body, wrapped in plastic sheeting, was well preserved, and the pathologist was able to take a sample of tissue from the liver and other organs. Tests at the laboratories at Scotland Yard proved conclusively that Ruby Baksh had died from a huge morphine overdose.

John Baksh had already been remanded in custody on a charge of the attempted murder of Madhu. At first he had denied the charge but later in his cell he had pleaded guilty. Nevertheless, there were, he implied, extenuating circumstances. 'I didn't want to kill her,' he is alleged to have told detectives. 'It was the animal in me which took over and made me do it,' he said. 'I took a knife to her throat. It was the bad in me.'

Now he was charged with the murder of his first wife.

Baksh's trial on charges of murder and attempted murder began at the Old Bailey on 9th December 1986. His defence was that his first wife had committed suicide and that his second wife's throat wound was the result of an accident. It was not an easy defence to present, but Baksh tried his best.

When on remand in custody for attempted murder Baksh had initiated an energetic campaign to persuade Madhu that what had occurred was all very unfortunate. 'My Dear Madhu, I am very sorry for what happened that I put a knife on your throat,' he had written to her, 'I did not know what I was doing. I apologise. Yours for ever, John.' This explanation was not as persuasive as he might have hoped, and his wife, unsurprisingly, was the principal witness against him. Seeking another ally from within the family, Baksh is alleged to have tried to explain away his behaviour in a letter to Madhu's brother: 'I think we all have split personalities, good and bad in us,' he wrote. 'Sometimes one prevails, sometimes the other. I did not want to kill her.' He went on to describe the alleged murder attempt as 'a storm in a tea cup'.

Nor was Baksh the only one to plead his case through letter writing. The jury heard of a letter from Ruby's sister, Janet Williams, who had written to say that three days before she died, Ruby had sent her a letter, saying that 'she was fed up with her life and was going to commit suicide'. The counsel for the prosecution then produced three letters which Mrs Williams had written from India, where she worked as a nurse. In one she had written, 'My advice to you is to think seriously before taking any steps. If there are chances of a patch up, let me request you to take back the charge you have made against him.' In another letter she had written, 'Take back the case. It will be good for all of you. Life will be back to normal soon.' Can Mrs Williams really have believed this? She described Dr Baksh, her former brother-in-law, as 'a very nice gentleman'. Mrs Williams's philosophical view was that Madhu ought to forget the whole business. In every family, she said, there is 'trouble and confusion'. How remarkable that John Baksh managed to persuade Mrs Williams to write in such terms.

The court learnt how in 1979 Madhu Kumar joined Baksh's practice, where Ruby was also a partner. From the outset Baksh showed how attracted he was to her, but, although her own marriage was nearly over and even though she found him undeniably charming, she resisted his advances. She did not wish for an affair with a partner's husband nor indeed with any married man. He was madly in love with her; he would leave his wife, he told her. Could he really leave her after 21 years? Yes, yes, for Madhu he could. What about his two children, Madhu had asked. And her own two children? But eventually Baksh's persistence was rewarded. In December 1982, Madhu's divorce now finalised, Baksh called on her at home. He had brought champagne; they kissed for the first time. A few days later, on December 23rd, he and Ruby left for a break in Spain.

On New Year's Day Madhu had a phone call from Spain. It was Baksh, his voice trembling and emotional. Ruby was dead, he told her, just this very morning. He said that when he woke up – they had been to a party the night before – Ruby was lying beside him, dead. The local doctor had called, Baksh told her, and had diagnosed a heart attack. The body, he said, had to be buried within 24 hours. In any case, Ruby had loved Spain. She would have wanted to be buried there, and so she would be. Within two weeks of his return from Spain, Baksh and Madhu went through a private Hindu ceremony of marriage in her house. He gave her Ruby's wedding ring.

In May 1983 the couple went to Paris for a weekend. In bed one night at the Montparnasse Parc Hotel, Baksh began to weep. He confessed to murdering Ruby in Spain. He told her how he had spiked her bedtime drink with sleeping tablets. When she fell into a deep sleep he had injected a massive dose of morphine into her thigh. The Spanish doctor had needed no convincing by a fellow doctor that she had died of a heart attack.

'I felt as though I had fallen from heaven to earth,' Madhu said in court. 'I felt a mixture of disbelief, fury and depression. I was in absolute turmoil. The man who I loved and I thought was so wonderful was actually a murderer. I was lying next to him. He simply turned over and went to sleep, snoring.' She had been bewildered by such a remarkable admission. Her first reaction to the confession had been to run out of the hotel bedroom and shout out what she had heard. Why had he done it, she asked him over and over again. Always the reply came that he had committed the murder so that he could marry her. But what if he should now treat her in the same way as Ruby? Madhu had wondered, going over the events in the succeeding days and weeks. Ought she to tell someone – the police? Ruby's family? But who would believe such a preposterous story? And whenever she challenged Baksh, he would invariably answer, 'How can you be so cruel? What I have done is the biggest sacrifice anyone can do for love.' Madhu loved him deeply, and she had no doubt that he loved her. Despite her misgivings, they now went through a civil wedding ceremony.

Money was always important to Baksh. Police investigations revealed that he had been investing significant sums in insurance policies on Madhu's life. In spite of their joint annual income of £90,000, Baksh was heavily in debt. There was an income tax demand for £7,000, a bank overdraft of £2,000, a bill for school fees totalling about £2,000 and a substantial mortgage. In the event of Madhu's death, there would be a payout of £315,000. It would have been a worthwhile investment, just as Ruby's had been, with a return of £90,000.

The prosecution outlined the sequence of events that had led to the attempted murder. On January 4th, after a day spent shopping for diamonds for Madhu, they had celebrated with champagne. It was then that she had felt herself slipping into unconsciousness. Baksh had put a sleeping draught into her glass. Then, when she was dazed, he had injected her with morphine in the back of the thigh. After this, he had driven her to Keston, where he partially concealed the body in the bushes, and slit her throat with a kitchen knife. He had driven away and then, realising that he had left a glove by Madhu's body, he had gone back to retrieve it. 'I found her still breathing but something stopped me from stabbing her again,' he is alleged to have told police.

It had been a carefully conducted plan. After leaving Madhu's bleeding body, Baksh had reported her missing to the police. He reported also that the BMW was gone, but the truth is that he had abandoned the car earlier in the day in Bromley. Even the cutting of her throat had been done with precision. Savage though the injuries were, Baksh had deliberately not severed any major arteries. He wanted her to survive for a number of hours after she had been reported missing. The next day a pathologist could have offered only an approximate time of death and Baksh would have been able to say that at about that time he was talking to the police about her absence. All evening he played the distraught husband, while his wife lay hidden in the bushes at Keston, her life ebbing away for over seven hours. The longer she survived, the better for him, the more substantial his alibi. But he did not reckon on the cold being so intense, for it was this, causing the blood to coagulate, and the morphine injection, that served to delay clinical shock, which saved her. When Keith Corbett discovered Madhu she was near to death. In another 30 minutes John Baksh would have been safe.

In court Baksh cut an unconvincing figure with his specious explanations of events. He said that his first wife had really committed suicide but he had told Madhu that he had murdered her simply to prove the depth of his love for her. As for the attack on Madhu, Baksh explained how they had had an argument. His wife, in a rage, had threatened him with a kitchen knife but he had calmed her down. Later she had complained of a pain in her chest and he had given her morphine. Then they had decided that they ought to seek advice from friends about their marital situation and had gone to visit them. Baksh told how he had put the knife in his pocket to show to their friends. It would serve as evidence of how serious their problems were.

At Keston they had felt the need for fresh air, Baksh said, and they had got out of the car. Madhu had asked him where the knife was and he had taken it out of his pocket. 'I pointed it at her throat because I wanted her to know what it felt like to be threatened with a knife. She pushed at it with her left hand; it was the pressure of her hand that pushed the knife into her neck.' And so he had abandoned her. And that was the doctor's story.

But the jury members could not bring themselves to swallow what they had been told. John Baksh was found guilty of both murder and attempted murder and received sentences of life and 14 years. It was recommended that he serve a minimum of 20 years. He had committed one perfect murder and only by chance had failed in his attempt to commit a second.

After his arrest the police had scrutinised three other deaths. Baksh's 80-year-old mother, Martha, in good health in a private nursing home, suddenly fell ill after he had visited her, dying three days later. In May 1978, one of his partners, Dr David Jones, collapsed and died on a golf course in Spain. Five months later Dr John Groome, his other partner, collapsed and died. Until their deaths both men had been in good health. No conclusions were reached, for all of the bodies had been cremated. But the police had thought it not unreasonable to make these further enquiries. 'Dr Baksh was totally evil,' said DI Tom Hamilton. 'He openly told us he was in favour of euthanasia, not in the sense of a mercy killing but in the context that anyone who had outlived their usefulness should be disposed of.' Had Baksh's partners and his mother outlived their usefulness? Ruby certainly had. And so had Madhu.

A GREAT
DETECTIVE

---※---

Of course, Sherlock Holmes rather spoils it for real-life detectives. The truth is that in real life the pieces of crime jigsaws do not frequently lie about so obviously. So often, successful police work is the result of hard drudgery, perhaps with a slight admixture of luck. But sometimes there is that leap of the imagination which bridges the gap between the known and the not-known and makes the whole scattered illogical drama fall into place. Hitherto unknown characters suddenly emerge and the solution that only a short time before had seemed so elusive is found. The case of Dagmar Peters illustrates quite perfectly how two detectives, Superintendent Robert Fabian and his sergeant, Harry Reynolds, had that intuitive flash which suddenly allowed them to see quite clearly where they ought to look and where their murderer was to be found.

On the cold, damp and dismal morning of 31st October 1946, a woman's body was found lying in the bushes by the side of the busy A20, on Wrotham Hill on the Maidstone to London road. An unusually alert lorry driver had spotted a woman's shoe in the road and had been curious about it. There was something strange about a single shoe, he thought. He had come to a stop to have a look around and saw the body. He called the police.

Superintendent Frank Smeed of Kent CID was called to the site and was joined there by Professor Keith Simpson, the celebrated Home Office pathologist. The victim, a middle-aged woman, seemingly unmarried because she wore no wedding ring, had been strangled, but apart from a grazed cheek and some swelling of one of the eyelids she was otherwise not obviously injured. There were no bruises to her face, nor indeed to other parts of her body. Clearly she had put up no struggle: what had happened to her had been unexpected.

The woman's coat and stockings were torn. Her legs were scratched too. Simpson was able to assure Smeed that the marks on her legs were made after death. It was a reasonable conclusion that after her death, the woman had been dragged into the bushes at the roadside. There were no clues as to the woman's identity; there was no purse, no handbag, nothing which could tell them who she was. Nor were there any clues left by the murderer. Even the murder weapon, some sort of ligature, was nowhere to be found.

The post-mortem conducted that evening revealed that the woman had been murdered only a few hours before the discovery of her body. It was estimated that she had been killed between seven and nine o'clock that morning. The ligature round her neck had been pulled tight from behind for between 15 and 20 seconds. Sometimes pathologists can identify the nature of the ligature – rope, cord, bootlace, for example – but in this instance Simpson was uncertain. What he could see was that a piece of folded cloth had been used, for the impressions of the folds were clearly visible in four distinct blue ridges across the front of the woman's neck. The woman had not been sexually assaulted: she remained a virgin.

By now Fabian and Rawlings had been called from Scotland Yard to West Malling Police Station to conduct the investigation. They studied the scene of crime photographs. They too were of the view that the body had been dumped away from where the killing had taken place.

At this point Professor Simpson made his most valuable contribution, offering the view that when she died the woman was sitting upright and for a while after she had remained in that position. His conclusion arose from his observation of the post-mortem stains on her skin. Post-mortem lividity commences shortly after death, though it does not make itself obvious for three or four hours. What happens is that when the circulation ceases the blood settles into the lowest available vessels and imparts a vivid colour to the affected parts. The patches of lividity that Simpson noted suggested that she had been seated in a fairly hard seat, a seat rather less well upholstered than a car, perhaps a lorry. This early pointer set the investigation in a positive direction.

At once Fabian issued the following message to every police station in Britain. 'Urgent inquiry is requested. Trace any lorry on A20 road Wrotham Hill, Kent, between 5 and 8 am, 31st October

1946.' As a consequence of this there was in the next 24 hours a nationwide check on garages, haulage contractors, delivery firms and lorry drivers. It was a mammoth exercise but it produced no result.

The following morning the victim was identified as 47-year-old Dagmar Peters, a harmless, decent, somewhat eccentric woman, who lived on her own in Hever Avenue, Kingsdown, in what was described as either a hut or a small bungalow. Whether hut or bungalow, it was undeniably squalid. Her mother lived only yards away and distressed as she naturally was, she was able to fill in some of her daughter's background. Dagmar, her mother said, went once a week to London to visit her sister-in-law. She would rise at five o'clock and because she had little money would hitch-hike the 30 miles. So she was not the victim of a robbery, then.

Nevertheless some of her poor possessions were missing. Where was the key to her house and the brown attaché case that she always took to London with her sandwiches and perhaps some little gift for her sister-in-law? Where was her yellow string handbag? It was important to find these. The killer might have touched them, left some trace.

It was easy enough to find an identical key purse and have photographs published in the *Police Gazette* and the national daily papers, but the yellow string handbag? Then Fabian learnt that it had been crocheted for Dagmar by another of her sisters-in-law, who lived in Woking. At once Fabian despatched an officer to her house to explain the situation. Would she, could she, crochet another bag, identical to the missing one? Of course she would. And the bag was completed overnight.

By the following day its photograph appeared in the newspapers, and the result was astonishing. A 15-year-old, Peter Nash, on his father's farm at West Malling, was not unnaturally interested in the local murder and reading the account of the progress of the investigation was amazed to see the photograph of the bag. He had fished it up in Clare Park Lake only two days earlier. His father took him at once to the police station, where hopes were raised and as quickly dashed. No, he hadn't the bag now, he said. He'd given it away to a neighbour. Off to the neighbour, then, but, no, she didn't have it; as a matter of fact, she'd given it to someone else. And that someone else, when the police called, explained that she had also passed it on, but at last the bag was tracked down. It now transpired that in 48 hours, not

Dagmar Peters lived here by herself.

only had the bag been in the lake, but its three different lady owners had each washed it thoroughly. Nevertheless, at the Metropolitan Police laboratory, there was confirmation that this was Dagmar's bag for one hair belonging to the murdered woman and another from her dog were found still attached.

This clue did not immediately bring the investigators any nearer to the truth; nor, for that matter, did the discovery the following day of a torn-up piece of the cardboard attaché case on the side of the A20. The meticulous search of the verges and hedges of the road produced similar fragments. The driver had shredded the case, presumably by hand, desperate to be rid of evidence that might hang him.

Although 1,500 statements poured in to Fabian's officers from firms and lorry drivers throughout the country, none of these upon investigation was a likely candidate for suspicion. Fabian was worried that the initial impetus was dying. He needed some other lead, but the lack of success from the haulage industry was a matter of concern. In the early hours of the morning, neither of them able to sleep soundly in their hotel beds, Fabian and Rawlings talked matters over. They went over the whole investigation, point by point, but made no headway. It was beyond them, and they feared that the longer it took them the more likely it was that the murderer would escape. Something was missing – or they were missing something.

They began to discuss yet again the torn-up case and the yellow string handbag. Wasn't it odd, they mused, that the case was all along the road and the handbag was in the lake? Why, they wondered, had he taken the bag to the lake? But had he? They thought about it. The lake was at least 200 yards from the road. Would he leave his lorry by the side of the road and walk across a field to throw the bag into the lake? And if he did that with the bag, why not the same with the case? Then there was an eight-foot fence to climb to get to the lake. So, did Dagmar Peters' murderer leave his lorry, cross a field, climb a fence, all to throw her bag in a lake? It made no sense; and, if it made no sense to Fabian and Rawlings, it would just as likely make no sense to the murderer of Dagmar Peters.

So how did the bag get into the lake? By morning the policemen had an idea. It must have been thrown into a stream which fed the lake. It was a Guide Leader who told Fabian that the old mill stream at East Malling ran partly underground to the lake. Investigations moved to the old mill, now a cider factory, where, from a roadside bridge, the two policemen began throwing bottles into the water. Within an hour they found their bottles in the reeds of the lake. Good. Now for the ultimate test: Fabian took his vital piece of evidence, the much travelled, much washed handbag, and threw it into the mill stream. Three hours later he found it floating at the edge of the lake. The murderer had been here; Fabian sensed it. He knew he was close to the man he sought. The lorry had been here, calling at the cider works.

But again Fabian's hopes were dashed. Not one of the 1,500 lorries in the area on October 31st that had been checked mentioned a visit here. Presumably, the driver had stopped his lorry, thrown away the string handbag, climbed back in the cab and driven off – another trail gone cold.

Then at the gate – and this is another of those inspirational leaps – Fabian spotted a pile of bricks. They had just been dumped there, and obviously dumped recently, for otherwise they would have been taken inside. When questioned the works foreman said that they belonged to a subcontractor doing some work at the factory. In his turn the subcontractor said that he was uncertain when they had been delivered. They had been brought by a haulage firm from Cambridge, he said.

Off to Cambridge went Fabian and Rawlings to call on the haulage firm. Yes, said the hauliers, one of their lorries, a four-ton Albion, had delivered bricks to the cider works on October 31st. Why had they not said so when asked by the police, Fabian asked: they had held up the enquiry into a murder. The hauliers, however, had an answer: the police had not come to see them. The firm's premises straddled the boundary of the Cambridge city and the county police forces, and each had assumed that the other had made enquiries in response to Fabian's message. It must have been a chance in a million. This was perhaps the only firm in the country not to have been checked during the enquiry. And it was the very firm which employed the murderer of Dagmar Peters.

The driver, Fabian was told, had left the firm only days after the murder. His name was Sydney Sinclair and he was still living locally. Sinclair was contacted and asked to present himself at Cambridge police station. The Criminal Records Office could produce no information about Sinclair, but, as soon as the burly, tough looking driver walked into the interview room, Fabian sensed that he was looking at a man who had served time in prison. Was it the way he held his cigarette? Was it the guarded look as he came in the room? There was something which alerted the policeman.

In his book, *Fabian of the Yard*, the detective describes what happened next. It offers another example of the intuitiveness of a very subtle officer.

'"What did you say your name was?" I asked sternly. He shuffled, discomfited. "It's ... Sinclair."

"Come on! How long has it been Sinclair?" I was bluffing. In the silence his gaze dwindled down from my face to the floor. "It's Hagger," he said solemnly. "Harold Hagger."'

While the interview proceeded another enquiry was sent to the Criminal Records Office. Harold Hagger, it transpired, had 16 convictions, including an assault on a woman.

Hagger admitted to being on the A40 at the time of the murder and he had delivered bricks to the cider factory. He had left them at the gate. Fabian told Hagger that pieces of the attaché case and a paper bag belonging to the dead woman had been found in Winterfield Lane on the road to London. The driver admitted finding the case. He had destroyed it; he had thrown it in pieces out of the window as he drove along. No reason for that – he'd just destroyed it.

Then Fabian took the suspect out in a police car along the route. At one point Hagger pointed out of the window towards the roadside hedge. That, he said, was about where he threw the vest. The vest? Fabian was stumped. What vest? The woman had been fully clothed when she was found, but the police car was stopped and the hedge searched. And there it was, a man's vest. Dagmar's mother was asked about it. Her daughter had bought it at Maidstone two days before she died, and on that cold morning she had worn it round her neck as a scarf – well, it was a cold day. When the scarf was examined further it was found that the texture of the cloth matched the ridge marks on Dagmar's neck. It was the ligature Fabian and Rawlings had been seeking.

Hagger then explained what had occurred. He had stopped to give Dagmar a lift, but not far along the main road he had driven off into a lane. It was then, he said, that she tried to steal his wallet. Angry, he had tried to frighten her. It was all an accident. 'I didn't mean to kill her,' Hagger said. 'I must have pulled the scarf too tight.'

Where was his jacket at the time, Fabian asked him. Hagger said it was hung up in the cab and Fabian queried this. The cab, on that cold morning, must have been freezing, for it had no heating. And yet, here was Hagger claiming to be driving in his shirt sleeves. Fabian could not accept that, nor could the jury.

Hagger was hanged at Wandsworth on 18th March 1947, caught out by a first-class pathologist and two detectives, Fabian and Rawlings, on top form.

THE GREAT
BULLION ROBBERY

There is no mystery now about the Great Bullion Robbery, but at the time it puzzled police and authorities in both England and France. How could over £12,000 worth of bullion – estimated at today's valuation at £1.5 million – just disappear in the course of its journey from London Bridge to Paris? The system was thought to be foolproof, but the robbers came (how?) and went (again, how?) with two hundredweight of gold and coins. It seemed an insoluble mystery.

The facts? At 8.30 on the evening of 15th May 1855, the mail train left London Bridge station en route for Dover via Redhill, Ashford, and Folkestone. At Folkestone, a bullion consignment in three iron-bound boxes was removed from the safe in the guard's van and taken to the quay to be shipped to Boulogne and then on to Paris. It was at Boulogne when the three boxes were weighed that the first alarm was raised. One box weighed 40 pounds less than it had weighed in London. The two others weighed slightly more. Nevertheless, the boxes went on to Paris. Again they were weighed and the discrepancy confirmed. When the boxes were opened, they were found to be filled with small bags containing lead shot. The accusations of police and railway authorities flew back and forth across the Channel. It was a mystery that would not be solved for 16 months.

By then it had turned from a great mystery story into a tale of bitter revenge. Two different men, both seeking revenge at different times, blew the case wide open.

Shortly after this most remarkable robbery, a tall dark, somewhat genteel looking man – silk top hat, fancy waistcoat, well fitting frock coat – proved rather attractive to 19-year-old Emily Campbell, living at that time with William Humphries, who was described variously as auctioneer, estate agent and pimp. In all likelihood he combined each of these callings. When Emily, who till then had called herself Mrs Humphries, went off with the urbane, obviously well-heeled interloper, and now called herself Mrs Adams, Humphries, outraged at his loss, determined to avenge himself.

Humphries knew enough about the man who had cuckolded him; he knew that he was not called Adams; he knew that he was not called Jenkins either, though some addressed him as such. He knew that he was 40-year-old Edward Agar, a professional safecracker at the top of his profession. Humphries would bring him down; he had him arrested on what seems to have been a trumped-up charge of fraud and forgery. In January 1857 Edward Agar was sentenced to transportation for the term of his natural life.

Yet only 16 months before, Edward Agar had been the prime mover behind the mysterious Great Bullion Robbery and now he was in the hulks at Portland, awaiting shipment to New South Wales. But he never uttered a word about the remarkable exploit until he learnt that another of his lady friends, Fanny Kay, a Tunbridge girl, who had borne his child, had been left destitute. Edward Agar's criminal colleague, William Pierce, had salted away for himself the £3,000 of Consols and more which Agar had asked him to invest for Fanny and her baby.

William Humphries had had his revenge on Agar. Now it was Agar's turn to have his revenge on Pierce. He told the authorities exactly how that huge quantity of gold had been spirited away. In consequence, the 40-year-old Pierce and two others, William Tester, a 26-year-old railway clerk and James Burgess, a 35-year-old railway guard, stood trial at the Central Criminal Court in the second week of January 1857.

This trial excited great interest owing to the daring nature of the robbery, the ingenuity with which it had been planned and executed, the large sum involved, and the respectability of not only Burgess and Tester but of the principal witness, the convict Edward Agar. Young Tester, black moustached and heavily side-whiskered, stood in the dock, smartly dressed, a monocle dangling down the front of his waistcoat. Recently, Tester, from a highly respectable family, had left the South Eastern Railway Company's employ and had taken up a senior post with the Swedish railways. As for Burgess, who appeared in court in his railway uniform, there had never been the slightest doubt about his honesty.

Indeed, after the robbery, he had been questioned but had satisfied his questioners that he had had nothing to do with it.

The third character in the dock, William Pierce, was an altogether more louche character. Employed at one time by the South Eastern Railway as a ticket printer, he had, on account of his gambling, been invited to leave the company's employ. In recent years, he had scraped a precarious living on the turf. By 1854, when he renewed his acquaintance with Agar, who had returned from America with a bank balance of at least £3,000 – from 'speculation', he was to say – Pierce was destitute, much of his miserable property in hock. He had even asked Fanny Kay, whom he was later to betray, to lend him a shilling. Now he managed to dress rather better in Agar's cast-offs.

Sometime in 1854 Agar and Pierce talked over a matter that over the years they had discussed – how to steal one of the regular French-bound bullion consignments from the Dover mail. What they did know was that it would require inside help. Getting the safe keys was the problem. But they already knew Tester from the days when he was the station master at Margate and they knew Burgess too. Although neither man had previously engaged in criminal activities, they were persuaded to join them in the plan, persuaded that the risks were worthwhile.

The matters to be resolved must have seemed at first to be insurmountable. Bullion consignments were placed in iron-bound boxes. These were placed in an iron safe, secured by Chubb locks; then sealed, weighed and locked before leaving London Bridge. The safe was not opened until it reached Folkestone, where the boxes were transferred to a safe on the ferry. There were two locks to the safe and keys to these were kept in London, in Folkestone and also by the ferry captain, an employee of the South Eastern Railway Company.

A full year before the robbery Agar and Pierce were considering various options as to how to carry out their enterprise. In May 1854 they went to Folkestone, posing as holidaymakers, Mr Adams and Mr Packham, watching the trains, booking offices and clerks. They observed the arrival and departure of the bullion chests, saw that the safe key was locked in a cupboard, and noticed that the key to the cupboard was kept in the cash drawer.

It was on this trip that Agar 'smoked' the booking office lock. In the absence of the clerks who had gone to the quay when the boat arrived, Agar went to the locked door. He slid two slender half-cylinders of metal, blackened with carbon, into the lock so that between them they covered the central spindle. Then after a little expert jiggling, they were drawn out and the master cracksman could calculate the internal geography of the lock. He would make a key to the booking office.

In July, Agar learnt from Tester that for security reasons the locks on the safe were to be recombined at Chubbs. New keys, of course, would have to be made. Here is where Tester was useful. As the assistant to the Superintendent of Traffic, the whole of the business of contacting and making arrangements with Chubbs fell to him. In October Tester met Agar at a pub with the new key in his pocket. Agar made a wax impression of the key, but unfortunately Tester had not brought the second key. The task was only half complete.

Agar went off again to Folkestone, staying at the Pavilion Hotel. A man of enormous inventiveness, he had arranged for a box of three hundred sovereigns, addressed to C E Archer, to be sent from London Bridge to Folkestone. It travelled by train in the safe in which the bullion boxes were usually conveyed. At the Folkestone booking office, the clerk, having no suspicions of the London gentleman, opened the cupboard and took from it the safe key. He then left this very respectable gentleman alone in the office while he went to the safe in the guard's van. The clerk returned with 'Mr Archer's' property. He was unaware that in his absence the gentleman had taken a wax impression of the cupboard key.

Later in the year, Agar and Pierce returned to the Kent coast, putting up this time at the Rose Inn in Dover. One evening they walked across the heights to Folkestone, arriving at the station before the mail train came in. They knew that there was always bustle and confusion at this time, and that the two clerks were frequently absent for a very short time from the booking office. This evening, in their absence, Pierce in railway uniform opened the office with the 'smoked' key provided by Agar, opened the cupboard with the second key, also provided by Agar, took out the safe key, and handed it to Agar waiting outside. Agar took an impression and then returned the key to Pierce, who replaced it in the cupboard. The job was over in less than a minute.

The next task was to make keys from the wax impressions. Days were spent filing blank keys. And they had to be tested. Half a dozen times Agar accompanied Burgess to Dover in the guard's van, testing his keys on the safe until he was satisfied that they fitted the safe locks perfectly.

There was no point in robbing the safe when there was little in it, but Tester, right at the hub of railway traffic, was in a position to let the two robbers know when it would be worth their while. Sometimes gold to the value of £12,000 was on the train and Agar and Pierce decided to wait until such a consignment was on board. They calculated that £12,000 in gold would weigh about two hundredweight and that would be as much as they would be able to carry away.

In consequence they purchased an equal weight of lead shot, which they poured into cloth bags in quantities of four or eight pounds. These small bags of shot were put into four leather courier bags, which, concealed under a cloak, could be strapped close to the body. Agar also bought some carpet bags to be carried in the hand.

Now Agar moved into Pierce's house in Crown Terrace in Hampstead Road. Every night for a fortnight, they left Crown Terrace in a cab, carrying their carpet bags and with their courier bags on their backs. Night after night they took the cab to London Bridge station, waiting outside for a signal from Burgess who was to be contacted by Tester when there was a worthwhile consignment. At last, on May 15th, James Burgess casually strolled out of the station concourse, looked about, and wiped his face. That was the signal.

Now the two robbers, both cloaked, and Pierce also wearing a dark wig, went to the platform and coolly handed their carpet bags to a porter to stow in the guard's van. Pierce took a seat in a first-class compartment while Agar hung about the platform as if waiting for someone. Then, seeing the station master's attention diverted, he jumped into the guard's van with Burgess just before the train set off.

When the train started off at 8.30 pm, Agar was ready to empty the iron-bound boxes of gold, which had only hours before been entrusted to the South Eastern Railway Company. He opened the safe with his false key. Using a mallet and chisel he wrenched the iron clamps off the first box and then wedged it open. Out came the bars of gold, which were quickly weighed on Agar's scales before being placed into one of the carpet bags; back into the safe went the bags of shot. The iron clamps were replaced and new wax seals were attached to the box. At Redhill, 35 minutes after leaving London Bridge, the train made its first scheduled stop. And here along the platform came William Tester, carrying a little leather bag, just large enough to take some of the gold – so much less for Agar and Pierce to have to carry at their journey's end.

At Redhill, Pierce left his compartment and joined Agar and Burgess in the van. Now the second box was opened, this one full of American 'eagles', each worth five dollars. These were poured into the bags. The third box contained just too much for the men to carry. They took as much as they could manage. Agar and Pierce then went back to the first class compartment at a convenient stop, leaving the carpet bags in the van with Burgess.

By 10.30, when the train reached Folkestone, the boxes were back in the safe, the van was swept and everything made to look as normal as possible. Burgess, aided by porters, manhandled the bullion boxes, filled with lead shot, onto the platform.

At Dover, Agar and Pierce collected their carpet bags from the van, and each carrying nearly one hundredweight, went into the Dover Castle public house. They had a brandy – well-merited, perhaps – and then returned to the train due to leave for London at two o'clock in the morning.

At the barrier the ticket collector was a shade dubious. The two passengers had return tickets from Ostend. Had these bags been through customs, he asked. After all, he knew that the arrival of tonight's boat had been delayed. But Agar was sharp enough. Yes, of course they had come through customs, he told the collector, handing him a silver coin. They had come through the previous evening. He and his companion had spent the day in Dover. They were nodded through.

Arriving in London in the early hours, the thieves asked a cabman to take them to the Great Western railway station. He was later to comment on the weight of the bags, which he estimated at about a quarter of a hundredweight or more. Before reaching their destination they changed cabs three times before making their way on foot to Pierce's house in Crown Terrace. In the course of the day, they met Tester who handed over the gold he had collected at Redhill. Later, in money-changers' shops they disposed of more than 400 of the American 'eagles', for which they received about £420.

Agar and Pierce now moved to Agar's house at Cambridge Villas in Shepherd's Bush. Here, Pierce took some of his share. About 100 ounces of gold was cut off a bar and he sold this at £3

The Great Bullion robbers – Tester, Agar and Burgess.

an ounce. He also took the greater part of the American money and now had about £720 in total at his disposal. What a transformation in the fortunes of the seedy little down-at-heel gambler. He put it about that he had had a big win on 'Saucebox' in the St Leger.

But there was still serious work to be done. All marks of the origin of the gold had to be removed from the bars by melting it in a forge. Always full of ingenuity, the men erected a furnace in the first floor back bedroom of Agar's house. They took out the stove and replaced the stones on the base of the fireplace with fire bricks. Then, placing the gold in a crucible they stoked up the fire to about 1,240 degrees: only such a heat could melt gold. They carried this out, not without some danger to themselves and the house, over several days. When it was molten, the gold was poured into iron moulds about one foot long. Unsurprisingly, both men were always very hot and dirty. Fanny Kay, at the time still living with Agar, saw nothing but she did for several days hear a noise 'like the roaring of a large fire'. When she questioned the men, complaining of the excessive heat in the house, they told her that, like true Victorian entrepreneurs, they were weaving leather aprons. After the operations ceased the stove was replaced and blackleaded and all obvious signs of activity removed.

In the succeeding weeks Agar sold considerable amounts of gold to fences and was now extremely rich. As the summer wore on, however, he fell out with Fanny Kay. She was the mother of his child but she was a drunkard, and he tired of her. He moved to Kilburn, staying there in Pierce's new house for some weeks. It was here that the gold was now stored, in a hole dug in the pantry, from which they sold it piece by piece.

Life was good for the four men who had carried out the daring enterprise. No one could work out how the robbery had been committed. Pierce set himself up in a betting office near Covent Garden. Tester bought Spanish Bonds, and Burgess very sensibly bought Turkish Bonds, as the Crimean War was swinging along nicely – in financial terms, that is.

Then Agar, only weeks after his magnificent coup, took up with a new love, Emily Campbell. Humphries, her former lover, consumed with a desire for revenge, succeeded only three months after the robbery, in having his rival sentenced to life imprisonment. Yet Agar in the hulks remained silent while his erstwhile colleagues in the great unsolved criminal enterprise saved and spent and anticipated a life free from financial care for ever.

But then Fanny Kay received a letter from Agar asking her to buy a silver cup for their baby and one for Pierce's child also. She could not afford it, she told him. But he had left money in trust for her; Pierce was supposed to be looking after her. Was he not? No, she was destitute. Pierce had given her very little; he had even thrown her out of her house. And so the whole business unravelled in the Central Criminal Court.

After a three day trial, the jury retired for only ten minutes. All three accused were found guilty. The judge, Mr Baron Martin, speaking of Agar described him as 'a man who is as bad, I dare say, as bad can be, but that he is a man of most extraordinary ability no person who heard him examined can for a moment deny... It is obvious that he gave to this and, perhaps, to many other robberies, an amount of care and perseverance one-tenth of which devoted to honest pursuits must have raised him to a respectable station in life, and considering the commercial activity of this country in the last 20 years, would probably have enabled him to realize a large fortune.' Although Agar had brought to light what had happened on the mail train, there was to be no remission of his sentence.

The judge despised Pierce most of all, not for his part in the robbery, but for his betrayal of Fanny Kay and her child. While he must have accumulated perhaps as much as £15,000, he took it for himself. 'This you stole and appropriated to your own use,' the judge said. 'It is a worse offence, I declare, than the act of which you have just been found guilty. I would rather have been concerned in stealing the gold than in the robbery of that wretched woman – call her harlot, if you will – and her child. A greater villain than you are, I believe, does not exist.' *The Times* reported: 'This strong language was received by the audience with a loud burst of applause.' The judge regretted that Pierce, guilty only of 'simple larceny' could be given hard labour for no more than two years, including three months in solitary confinement. 'I am unfortunately compelled to inflict a punishment less severe than upon the other prisoners. They were servants of the company and you were not.'

The respectable first offenders, Burgess and Tester, who had stolen from their employers, were sentenced to transportation for a term of 14 years. 'You were willing to play the game,' Mr Baron Martin told them. 'You must pay the forfeit.'

The bonds that Agar had asked Pierce to be used for Fanny's benefit were judged to have been his private property before the robbery, and other monies, including his share of the robbery which he had given to Pierce, were legally handed over to Fanny. After all Agar had not been charged with robbery – what irony.

There have been other great train robberies in this country and abroad, but, for the sheer silkiness of the non-violent operation, the absolute panache with which it was carried out and its conclusion, this one takes some beating.

THE WREN CASE

———————— ❁ ————————

It is a baffling little murder, this business in Miss Wren's shop. It is not, by the way, intended to diminish such a dreadful matter by calling it 'little'. It is just that in the bloody annals of murder this case seems so slight, so insignificant. Yet, 70 years after the old woman's shocking death, the case is still recalled, still retains its power to fascinate. Of course it is not simply that this was an unsolved murder; its interest does not so much lie in the motive or even the identity of the perpetrator. What is constantly compelling about this murder is the attitude of the woman to the police and magistrates and others who, until she finally succumbed five days after the attack, tried to persuade her to identify her attacker. But she would not. The stubborn 81-year-old, savagely battered and bruised, either concealed the identity of the man (yes, a man – that much she conceded) or made misleading statements. She had five days in which to let her interrogators know who was responsible for her appalling situation, but to the end her answers were unhelpful and still at this distance in time it seems that they were deliberately so.

'Miss Wren - General Stores', so the plaque outside the door read. It was just an ordinary terrace house in Church Road, Ramsgate, with one deep step up to the front door. Inside, quaint perhaps even in 1930, the interior was dark, the shelves a jumble of fly papers, Sunlight soap, bottles of dolly mixture and liquorice allsorts, Zebo for cleaning the grate, bundles of firewood, Mansion polish, Bird's custard powder, all penny-twopenny stuff here, where the business of buying and selling was transacted in gloom and grime. Miss Margery Wren, with her late sister, now just four years dead, had run this shop for longer than most hereabouts could remember. Gladstone was still prime minister when the Wren girls first started. They conducted business during the old queen's golden jubilee and they were serving customers in the days of the war against the Boers. The two women continued their modest trading throughout what they knew as the Great War. The partnership ended in 1926 with Mary Jane's death and, after 50 years and more, the Wren association with the Church Road shop finally concluded with the attack on its remaining owner late in the afternoon of Saturday, 20th September 1930. It occurred only an hour or so after the old woman was seen brushing her front step, not more than a half hour before 11-year-old Ellen Marvell came on an errand for her mother, seeking a packet of blancmange powder. But the door was locked and that seemed odd to Ellen, for she had been here countless times, often later than this. Miss Wren, she knew, was always open at six o'clock. So Ellen rattled at the door, banged it with her knuckles, and called out Miss Wren's name. Her patience was eventually rewarded, though she was astonished at what she saw when the old woman staggered to the door.

'Blood was streaming down both sides of her face,' Ellen told the police. 'I said, "Whatever is the matter?" and she asked me what I wanted. I had to tell her several times that I wanted blancmange powder before she understood. She then took all the blancmange powders from a shelf and told me to take whatever flavour I wanted. She did not tell me what was the matter.'

Worried about the condition of Miss Wren, who would not say what had occurred, Ellen ran home to tell her parents. Her father went at once to the still open shop where he found the shopkeeper in a collapsed state on a chair in the kitchen, a grim little room, lit by a single candle. She had had a fall only 15 minutes or so earlier, Miss Wren explained. Mr Marvell, concerned, sent for both the police and a doctor.

Dr Archibald, who had tended the Wren sisters for

Margery Wren. (Kentish Express)

several years, arrived shortly before the police. He was appalled at the extensive bruising on the old woman's face, the abrasions to the front and side of her neck, the eight lacerations to her head and the broken rib. Though not known at that stage – it was Sir Bernard Spilsbury who revealed this at the post-mortem – there were fractures in and around the windpipe, where she had been fiercely grabbed. It was impossible for her to have come by such injuries simply by falling. In his subsequent report, Dr Roche Lynch, the Home Office analyst, observed that two of the head wounds corresponded exactly in the distance from one to the other to the knobs on the fire-tongs. Miss Wren's first words to Dr Archibald were 'I am suffocating', and then she became increasingly distressed. She had had a giddy spell, she said, and then she told a different tale. 'He caught me by the throat,' she said, 'and then he set about me with the tongs.' The fire-tongs, bloodied, lay on the floor. Archibald then urged her to describe her assailant. 'You will never get him, doctor. He has escaped.' It was as though she had already decided that he should escape, that his pursuers would have no help from her.

The police, now in attendance, were convinced that there had been an attempted robbery and began a search of the premises, but they must have wondered if Miss Wren was worth robbing. The house was squalid and she evidently lived in poverty. Indeed at times she had pleaded poverty, often calling for bowls of soup from the next door soup kitchen. It was unlikely that she made much profit in her shop. There was no till, no accounting system, no record of takings. Behind the counter, police officers found a number of tins containing coppers and silver; perhaps the thief had been unaware of them. On the other hand, he had been aware enough of the house to lock the shop door and then make his escape through the back yard. Perhaps he had been frightened off before he could help himself to the tins containing the cash. Perhaps the sight of his victim, lying helpless on the floor, with the blood streaming down her face had terrified him. Had he come in with no intention of hurting her? Had things got out of hand? She was known to be strong-willed. Had she stood up to him when he went in to rob her?

Miss Wren was taken to Ramsgate Hospital and here she lingered for five days. She drifted in and out of consciousness, sometimes making rambling accusations to nurses and police about an assailant but then contradicting what she had said. On other occasions it had been an accident: she had tripped over the fire-tongs. And was there just one attacker? Or were there two? One day, delirious, she called out, 'Stop, stop, you are hurting me. You are a pair of heartless... You can't take it, you just can't take it.' Can't take what, these two? Her money?

To a policewoman by her bed Miss Wren confided, 'There were two of them set about me ... If I had not had my cap on they would have smashed my brainbox. One said, "Now I've got you I'll do you in." I was sitting in the armchair in the parlour when they came in. One grabbed me by the jaw from behind and threw me down and they both set about me. I did not really see them, only the wild eyes of one of them when he was smashing at my head. There was a knocking at the door and then they made their escape.'

At the inquest Dr Archibald mentioned that in one of Miss Wren's accounts her attacker was a big man with a red face, moustache and staring eyes. Later she amended this description, saying that he had no moustache but that he had an accomplice, who had stood at the door. There were three fellows on one occasion, four on another. Where did the truth lie?

Even though the police were unable to confirm that anything had been taken, so disorganised were the shop and the living quarters, the most plausible reason for the brutal attack on Miss Wren would seem to be that a robbery was intended. There was talk in the neighbourhood – talk which presumably had circulated without much foundation over the years – that Miss Wren, despite her appearance, despite her pleading poverty, was really very wealthy. It is the sort of assumption which so often leads to the old being attacked in their homes. Their impoverished appearance is only, some might think, because they are misers, with money hidden somewhere in the house. The reason they look so poor is that they won't spend their nest eggs. That is the logic behind many such attacks. But then Miss Wren added to the stories herself, encouraging speculation about her means. One day she was poor, another wealthy. She had told some people that she kept several hundred pounds in the shop or in the living quarters. She hinted at money hidden in an upstairs cupboard and in the gas oven. The tins that she always resorted to in her shop dealings must have more or less confirmed this idea in some minds. Furthermore, there was what her sister had left her in her will. Then there was talk about her property, six houses in London had been mentioned. A relative, a Mr Cook, told the police that he believed that she had owned these six houses but had sold them just over a year ago. He thought the money was invested. The truth is that Miss Margery Wren exaggerated her means. She had a small profit – a really small profit – from her really small shop. And from her sister's estate she received an annual sum of £13; even in 1930 it was a pitiably small sum.

On the Monday, the third day after the attack, officers from Scotland Yard were summoned to Ramsgate, for it was clear that this was shortly to turn into a murder enquiry. Chief Inspector Walter Hambrook, head of the Flying Squad, accompanied by Detective Sergeant Carson, arrived the following Wednesday. They learned of the Lowestoft man to whom she intended to lend a large sum of money – £1,900, it was said – to buy a trawler, but who he was remained a mystery. He was never traced. Did he ever exist? Then there was the businessman in Herne Bay, who, she claimed, had called on her and who, before setting about her with the tongs, had tried to borrow £10. Apparently this man did exist and had been seen in Ramsgate on the day of the murder, but when police enquired it was confirmed that he had left Ramsgate in the early afternoon, before Miss Wren was attacked. Another man, in Dover, was mentioned but he too was exonerated.

What seemed to be a promising clue, the discovery of a lady's handkerchief on the shop floor, came to nothing. And after such high hopes, for it had the name G F Davey written in marking ink in one corner. The police appeal in local newspapers, asking her to come forward, produced no result.

At other times from her hospital bed Miss Wren returned to the story of tripping over the tongs, denying that she had any enemies and saying that no one had hit her. Hambrook was quite convinced that she knew her assailant. Could she, for some obscure reason, be shielding someone? But why would she wish to do so? This was baffling. It was clear that she would not live long now, would never stand up in a witness box and point out her attacker. It was decided to give her the opportunity to make a dying declaration. Such a statement, from a death bed, may be acceptable as evidence in court. It is thought that the prospect of impending death is sufficiently awesome to elicit the truth, that the imminent passage through the gates of heaven is enough to produce a declaration equivalent to a statement made on oath. Such a statement, valuable in a case such as this, is exempt from the rules normally governing hearsay evidence. But the stubborn Miss Wren, though she now admitted that she knew her assailant, would not name him to the magistrate at her bedside. 'I do not wish to make a statement,' she said. 'I have seen my doctor and vicar. I have had communion. I know I am going home and do not wish him to suffer. He must bear his sins. There has been a misunderstanding.' At that she lapsed into unconsciousness and never recovered.

Five days after the attack, Miss Wren, a woman of undoubted iron constitution and indomitable will, left this life and left the police with a tangle of tales to follow up, none of which led anywhere. She had never given a coherent account of what happened to her.

Why did Miss Wren, in pain, in acute discomfort, not name the person, or persons, who had so brutally used her? She was aware that she was a murder victim. Why did she wish to shield her murderer? Why did she name half a dozen people, most of whom, perhaps all of whom, must have been innocent. Was it malice? Delirium? At the inquest the coroner, Dr Hardman, was to express his bewilderment and frustration at how matters had turned out. 'The greatest difficulty in this case,' he said, 'has been caused by the attitude of the dead woman herself. She made a number of varying and conflicting statements. At first she explained her injuries had been due to an accidental fall. At a later time she spoke of assaults committed, not by one person, or by two, but by three or four persons separately. The names of those persons were mentioned and allegations made against them. These statements raised a very difficult problem. It is perfectly obvious that some of these persons are entirely innocent and unconnected with the offence. It is quite likely that all of them are innocent, but their names have been mentioned. The evidence is bound to create painful feelings among a number of persons but I have very carefully considered what is the proper attitude of a coroner and jury. It is not at all improbable that she realised what she was saying, and the underlying reason why she made these statements was that she was endeavouring to shield some person she knew, and whom she wished to protect.'

The Chief Constable of Ramsgate, S F Butler, indicated his difficulties to the coroner. There were still three possible suspects on his list. He referred to A, B and C, who had complete alibis; there were, however, some doubts about the stories offered by D,

E and F, but at that point he was in no position to make an arrest
– and he never was.

At the inquest a verdict was returned of wilful murder against a
person or persons unknown. And so that verdict stands today.

In one account of the murder there is a footnote which says that
after Miss Wren's death a rumour circulated that she had given
birth to an illegitimate son and that it was he who had attacked
her. If true, it would explain her reluctance to name her assailant.
But again it does suggest simply our desire to have a proper
ending to our stories, to the stories that we always invent to
explain the details of other people's lives, to fill in those
inexplicable gaps.

In her lifetime, Miss Margery Wren was scarcely known beyond
the streets of Ramsgate where she continued into old age to run
her little general dealer's shop. Now she crops up in a variety of
books dealing with murder but her name is not known simply
because of what was so foully done to her: she is recalled for her
astonishing determination to keep a secret. But what was the
secret behind the secret? Small wonder that Walter Hambrook
called her the most determined, inflexible woman he had ever met.

THE LEY LINE
MYSTERY

———————— ❁ ————————

You start in Cannon Street in Dover. You start in fact at St Mary's church, not far from where it nudges shoulders with, among others, Thomas Cook, the kebab shop, the British Heart Foundation and the bookies. It's a quite ordinary beginning for the journey, and of course you need neither walk nor drive – not if you don't wish to. Instead get out a 1:50000 Ordnance Survey map (Sheet 179, to be exact) and you'll be able to follow the route north to Woodnesborough and its church. It's only a matter of ten miles, no great distance, but nevertheless there is something quite odd about this route.

You'll see that after leaving Dover the road passes through Church Whitfield and next through Ashley. Further north, you come to Betteshanger and then to Eastry, finally arriving at St Mary's church in Woodnesborough. Now, the interesting thing is that, although the road is not absolutely straight, the churches at Dover, Betteshanger, Eastry and Woodnesborough are all more or less in line; four churches, all in a row. Remarkable? Or just coincidence? Do you imagine that those old church builders seven or eight hundred years ago aimed to line up the churches?

The fact is that Kent is criss-crossed with churches aligned in this way. There are, for example, seven churches in a line from Southfleet to Halling and then along the North Downs to Charing. This covers a distance of 25 miles. There's no visible line, of course. At times there is a road or track to follow but at other times the line ignores the twists and turns of the road and barges on through fields and hedges, and up hills and down, till it reaches its 'marker'. Along some of the lines in the county, the markers are prehistoric burial mounds and old wells, Roman forts and earthworks, the villas of wealthy Romanised Britons, ruined castles and standing stones. Strange, isn't it?

To take another example. From Burham church, you can draw a line on the map to St Mary's church at Thurnham. This route takes you through the White Horse Stone and on to the scattered remains of the ancient burial mound at Little Kit's Coty, alternatively named the Countless Stones. Continue on the same line, following the Pilgrims' Way, and you'll come to Boxley church and then Detling church and finally, after about four and a half miles, you will reach Thurnham church. Was there something deliberate about the siting of these churches and the 4,000-year-old burial mound?

Let's examine a couple more of these lines before we start to consider what it is we are seeing. At Wrotham there's a prehistoric mound which is where this ten-mile line begins – or where it ends. It takes off in the direction of Trottiscliffe church and then arrives at the atmospheric, mysterious Coldrum Stones, where the breeze soughs through the branches of the trees. This is another of those old burial mounds, dating from about 2000 BC; the soil is now all eroded so that its bared grey stones stand up to the elements. From here the line goes in the direction of Birling church, after which it passes through the site of a Roman villa. From there it strikes out to Eccles church and after that to Kit's Coty House, Kent's principal prehistoric burial mound, which has powerful associations with magic. That is seven markers all in a line.

By the way, there are tales of spectral black dogs haunting the section of the Pilgrims' Way above Trottiscliffe and the Coldrum burial chamber. Indeed, many of the old sites throughout the country, often along ley lines, have associations with such mysterious animals.

John Timpson, in his book *Timpson's Leylines*, pointed out the line from Northbourne to Tolsford Hill. It begins at St Augustine's church, travels south-west to St Pancras's church at Coldred and then goes on through the chapel ruins at St John's Farm, over the White Gate crossroads, ending 14 miles later among the prehistoric mounds on Tolsford Hill.

To recap, then: invisible lines, seemingly linking prehistoric sites, Roman remains and medieval churches are found all over Kent. In fact they are found all over Britain and all over the world. Was there some great plan in all of this? Are these lines intentional? If they are it does seem that the original planners lived in prehistoric times, anything up to 5,000 years ago. But could they plan with such accuracy, so that sites miles apart,

Kit's Coty, Kent's principal prehistoric burial mound. (Centre for Kentish Studies)

could line up exactly? Could they align their sites with such precision? Of course they could. We tend to underestimate the skills of our ancestors living so long ago.

Stonehenge, that vast, complex astronomical calendar, was erected over a period of 1,400 years, between 3000 BC and 1500 BC. Its creators had the engineering skills to transport and erect the stones; they had the surveying and astronomical skills to place the stones so that once a year, on Midsummer Day, the sun's first rays hit the altar stone. This remarkable structure is also aligned to lunar cycles as well as the midwinter solstice on December 21st. The people who put up Stonehenge are unlikely to have been fazed by a simple matter of lining up earthworks, wells, and burial mounds across the landscape. Similar peoples, again without metal technologies, created similar lines in many other parts of the world.

As far back as the 18th century scholars had pondered the alignments in Britain, but it was not until 1921 that Alfred Watkins, a Herefordshire businessman and amateur archaeologist, presented a theory on the alignments. One summer's day, out in rural Herefordshire, he stopped his car to admire the view. There was a moment of revelation. It suddenly struck Watkins, on studying his map and the actual landscape in front of him, that so many features – standing stones, circles, burial mounds, hill forts, earthworks, moats, springs, wells, fords, castles – appeared to be in line. It was incredible.

Watkins wrote later that he 'followed up the clue of sighting from hill top to hill top ... found it yielding astounding results in all districts, the straight lines passing over and over again through the same class of objects'. He went on to expound his theories about the lines in lectures and in his book, *The Old Straight Track*, published in 1925. Watkins was of the view that tracks had been mapped out by surveyors in prehistoric times as a guide for traders. He concluded that men at this time, using surveying poles, had set out arrow-straight tracks, cutting through dense forests and following the line straight up hillsides and across rivers and marshes. They had not diverted from the line and had ignored whatever obstacles lay in front of them.

Watkins named these tracks *leys*, a word he borrowed from the Anglo-Saxons, for whom it signified a woodland clearing. He was aware that *ley* appeared frequently in place-names along the lines: Boxley, Pluckley, Ashley, Hastingleigh, Horselees are but a few examples in Kent. Not every ley place is on a ley line, but many are. It was not of course the Anglo-Saxons who created the first clearings in heavily wooded England. According to Watkins, they had been hacked out by the original surveyors, at least 2,000 years before the birth of Christ.

Along the tracks were sited burial places of chiefs and undoubtedly these were regarded as sacred places. Even more than 2,000 years after they were established, the pagan peoples continued to regard them as sacred. Romans undoubtedly surfaced some of the tracks, and remains of a Roman road are found on the ley line between Dover and Woodnesborough. Romanised Britons, doing well out of the Roman occupation, built villas on older sacred sites like that between Eccles and Birling, presumably believing that such locations would bring them good fortune. Later, when Christianity was being established in England in the 7th and 8th centuries, churches were frequently deliberately built on the old sacred sites. This is the manner in which the Christian Church colonised pagan England.

The straight lines are not in dispute, but Watkins' suggestion that they were to help traders to find their way across unknown territories does not hold water. Imagine it – walking in a straight line, never deviating for marshland, deep, fast flowing river, or steep incline. That is not the way that traders walk, nor anyone else for that matter. People find the easy way round obstacles. In Peru, Bolivia and Costa Rica, there are similar ley lines, often hundreds of miles long and straight as an arrow's flight. They too cannot have been tracks exclusively for walkers.

Let's have another look at a ley line. There is a lengthy one of about 30 miles that begins at Pegwell Bay, passing through the churches of St Mary at Wingham, St Peter at Bridge, All Saints at Petham, St Mary at Crundale, St Gregory and St Martin at Wye, and St Mary at Kennington. This ley goes on as far as Betherden, where it passes close to the church and then it simply ends. But do you see the point? A straight line, begun presumably in very ancient times, in some way linking locally significant places, and refreshed in the last thousand years by the placing of medieval churches.

For what reason were these alignments made? In the 1960s it was argued that they were related to UFOs. It was the view of some ufologists that UFO pilots flew along magnetic lines of force linking the ancient sites, which also acted as navigation features. They were in effect UFO flight paths. This is a theory which is also difficult to support. Even confirmed ufologists have expressed their doubts about this, recognising that if UFOs have enough navigational know-how to find their way here from outer space or from wherever it is they come, they are likely to be quite sophisticated enough not to have to rely on markers such as churches, stone circles, earthworks and the remains of Roman villas.

Others have advanced the view that leys mark lines of energy. In 1997 Kevin Carlyon, High Priest of The Covenant of Earth Magic – he is what would commonly be called a white witch – was asked to purify the Post Office Counters distribution centre at Aylesford, where staff seemed to be experiencing more than an unfair share of bad luck. Kevin charged crystals at Kit's Coty House before placing them at strategic positions within the building. He believed that the sequence of misfortunes which had befallen the staff over several months was because the building had been receiving a negative stream of ley energy, and he sought to eliminate this with a purer, more positive, energy form.

Many now consider that the lines are part of the ceremonial rituals performed by the shamans – the witch doctors and priests – active in early societies and still operating in some parts of the world. Shamans were the intermediaries between the tribe and the spirit world. They interceded on behalf of their tribal members, and concerned themselves with hunting and farming activities, with healing and with the souls of the dead. Their role was to explain the fundamentals – such as death, the after-life and the future – and how to ensure good fortune and escape ill-fortune.

Anthropologists describe shamans undergoing a symbolic death by going into a trance, most likely after taking hallucinatory drugs which promoted the sensation of spirit flight. This is how they claimed to enter the spirit world. While there they travelled along the same path as the spirits of the dead. This shamanic 'flight of the soul' seems to have been experienced as straight and arrow like and then symbolically imposed on ancient landscapes, perhaps as tracks or by sacred sites placed in a line. Placing burial mounds, earthworks and wells in line was perhaps some kind of symbolic representation either of death's journey or of the shaman's flight drawn out on the real landscape.

So then, let's take a final look at some other ley lines. From Pluckley's St Nicholas church the ley goes in the direction of Fir Toll, on to New House Farm and on then to the village of St Michael's, Cold Harbour Farm and Friezingham Farm. The Kent section ends after 14 miles at Castle Toll, the site of a Roman fortress, right on the border with Sussex, although the ley continues to Bexhill. There's another line of churches that runs for ten miles from St Leonard's at Deal and goes via St Mary's at Ripple, St Peter's at Whitfield, St Peter's at River, St Radegund's Abbey at Bradsole to the church of St Mary at Poulton. Imagine, 4,000 years ago, there was something powerful about this connected route, a line of sacred places, perhaps symbolically marking the routes of the spirits of the dead.

A remarkable trio of ley lines appear to pass directly through the church at Sowting, halfway between Folkestone and Wye. One line runs from Elmsted to Stanford; another from Hastingleigh to Postling, and a third from Bulltown to Lyminge.

What a fascinating mystery it is. What a remarkable continuity of thought; people down the ages, all linked by common concerns of life and death, of the past and the future, of ritual and prayer. That would seem to be the significance of ley lines, our link with the past communities of men and women whose fundamental preoccupations had a greater similarity to our own than we sometimes think.

It may now be a case for readers to have another look at the map and then get out their walking boots. There's a lot to puzzle over and much to wonder at along Kent's roads and footpaths, across her fields and woodlands.

Or there again, do the journeys at the kitchen table with your OS map spread out in front of you. A warm fire and a mug of tea and off you go.

THE LILY POND

———————— ❊ ————————

Definitely not the type. Definitely not, if you hold to the view that all murderers look evil and sinister. The fact is, however, that most of them have the disconcerting habit of looking just like the rest of the population – appallingly normal. And Charles Lewis, thin, besuited, wearing his pince-nez, not only looked ordinary, but he was ultra-respectable, ultra-reliable, a man with a responsible post in local government, the captain of the local bowls team, and a member of the Conservative party. His house in Erith Road, Belvedere was solid without being pretentious, a reflection of his own personality and character. His family life was as one might expect: he had been married for 30 years and he and his wife Maude had an adopted 19-year-old daughter, Freda, who was a *Titanic* orphan and a girl of whom they had every right to be proud. Lewis was 60-years-old and was looking towards retirement in a few years, with the prospect of more bowling and more gardening just over the horizon. No, on the face of it, Charles Lewis was not murderer material: assistant chief education officers rarely are.

So what a shock there was when the police dug up the unfinished fish pond in Lewis's back garden on the evening of Friday, 29th May 1931.

Lewis had rung Erith Education Office on the Wednesday morning – it had just reopened after the Whitsuntide break – to say that he was not coming into work that day. Then he had added: 'My wife and daughter are dead. I am going to them. Goodbye.' Without saying where he was calling from, he had then put down the receiver.

What could they make of such a telephone call – so abrupt, even taking the circumstances into account. Of course, he must have been very upset. And he was going to them, he had said. Did that mean that they had been involved in some accident over the holiday? Perhaps it meant that the two women had been away from Belvedere for the day and something terrible had happened to them. Perhaps there had been a motoring accident of some kind. Or did 'going to them' have another awful significance? Naturally, Frederic Evans, the Chief Education Officer, was disturbed by the call and made discreet enquiries, ringing hospitals and local newspapers, but there was nothing to explain what had occurred, no reports which linked up with the Lewis family.

That same morning, Lewis had called Stockwell Teacher Training College where Freda Lewis was on the point of completing her two-year course. She ought to have returned to the college on the Tuesday evening but would not now be back for a day or two, Lewis said. He would send a letter to explain her absence.

But it was the startling letter sent by Lewis to his brother-in-law in Wales which finally led police to the house, to the garden, to the fishpond.

This relative, unnamed for no obvious reason in reports of the case, had been so disturbed by the letter's contents that he had sent a telegram to Maude Lewis's step-brother, Frank Brown, an Uxbridge teacher, asking to meet him at Paddington Station the following day, Friday. Both men were seriously concerned about what Lewis had written, alarmed enough for one to travel to London from Wales and the other to take a day off work to meet him. Lewis's letter was later described at the inquest as 'very wild and apparently inconsistent and containing very disturbing news'. When they met, the men concluded that Lewis was suffering from delusions. Could what he had suggested in his letter be true? Were Maude and Freda dead? It was inconceivable, Brown said. He had heard from Maude recently. In fact, he had had a couple of letters from her – just cheerful family gossip really, talk about the weather, the garden, a proposed holiday – and Freda had written to him as well. She had waxed enthusiastic about a trip to the West Country, about her studies, about the dog, and about how her mother was delighted at plans for a fishpond in the garden. But Lewis's letter to his Welsh brother-in-law, that was a different matter altogether.

The two men, doubtless apprehensive, set off from Paddington for 37 Erith Road. And they cannot have been totally surprised that there was no answer to their knocks. Neighbours did express some surprise that the Lewises were not at home. Perhaps they had gone on holiday, they suggested, though usually, they said, they told each other when they were going to be away. And the

Maude Lewis.

dog, what about the dog? Whenever the Lewises went off they left the dog with a friend, but they had not done so this time.

It was clearly a matter for the police. Divisional Detective Inspector Thomas Cory from Blackheath was informed and he tried to trace relatives and friends but no one was able to cast light on the affair. Cory discovered that on the previous Saturday Lewis was at the bowling club and again on Whit Monday evening he was there watching play. All seemed perfectly normal, then. Had he been seen since? Yes, a neighbour had spotted him in the garden on Tuesday morning. And this seemingly was the last sighting of Charles Lewis.

Cory, sensing that this was undoubtedly a case of murder, called Superintendent Bill Brown, one of Scotland Yard's 'Big Five', telling him of the unusual circumstances. Brown was down at Erith early in the evening, and after a quick assessment of the situation decided that the house should be searched. Entrance was gained through an upstairs window. Inside everything appeared to be normal.

Freda Lewis

There were no signs of disorder, nothing to cause alarm; everything was tidy, everything in order. There were no dirty dishes in the scullery. The front room was being redecorated and the furniture, now covered with sheets, had been moved to the middle of the room. The three beds had been slept in but not remade and that was the only discordant note. If the Lewises had gone off on holiday would they have left the beds unmade? Nowhere, however, was there the suggestion of any kind of struggle: no bloodstain splashes on the floor or walls, no suggestive knives or blunt instruments, and certainly no bodies.

Brown peered out at the darkened garden and, seeing the fishpond, as yet unfinished and covered by green tarpaulin, ordered his team to bring out their spades. The small ornamental pond was kidney-shaped and measured about seven feet by four feet. The concrete base was two feet below surface level. The surface of the concrete had set hard but under the crust it was softer. Once the diggers had penetrated the concrete they came upon some resistance. It was three small sheets of corrugated iron, and under these, 17 inches below the concrete base, they discovered the bodies. Both women were dressed in nightclothes, each wearing a short woollen coat. They were completely wrapped in bed sheets, which covered body and face, and a piece of carpet.

Maude Lewis had bled from the right nostril, and her right eye was slightly bruised. Tied tightly under her chin was a blood-stained bath towel. Freda showed no signs of injury. With the two women was the family dog. All had presumably been done by night – the murder, dragging their bodies out into the garden and cementing them in.

Motive? That could wait. Now the search was on for Charles Lewis. Brown issued a brief description to be sent to police forces and newspapers nationwide: 'Sixty years of age, six feet in height, slim build, grey hair and eyes, gold-rimmed spectacles, walks with a limp suggestive of a withered leg.' See how ordinary, how absolutely commonplace he is. Perhaps the limp might be a giveaway, but for the rest Charles Lewis was as anonymous as any other white-collar worker in late middle-age.

On that same evening, at more or less the time when the bodies were discovered, Lewis made his last, typically understated, dramatic gesture. He had joined the ship *Royal Scot*, bound for Leith, at Wapping the previous day. He had booked his ticket in the name of Davidson. His doctor, he told the booking clerk, had recommended that he take a sea trip. On the Thursday he had stayed in his cabin but he was seen on deck on the Friday. But he kept himself to himself. Then, at 11 o'clock at night, he took a last turn about the deck and 14 miles or so off Whitby he disappeared over the side. There was an unsuccessful search for the body, which lasted an hour before the ship went on its way. Within hours the clothing left in the missing man's cabin was identified as Lewis's.

There were two inquests by the West Kent Coroner, the first of which, on June 2nd, dealt with little more than evidence of identity and the finding of the bodies. Sir Bernard Spilsbury had conducted the post-mortems on the previous Saturday and said that both women had been poisoned, but that it would take the analysts three weeks to decide which poison had been used. The second inquest, on June 30th, reached a verdict of murder against Charles Lewis. A local chemist, Ernest William Tapley, employed by Ascott's Pharmacies in Bexley Road, Belvedere, told the court that he knew Lewis well. On April 14th, the chemist said, Lewis purchased two and a quarter ounces of cyanide of potassium – as an insecticide, he had said – and a tin of Eureka weed killer. These were signed for in the poison book. It was the first time that Lewis, a regular customer, had bought poison.

There was further evidence from Frederic Evans, who spoke about Lewis's telephone call to the office; from Detective Inspector Cory, who described his enquiries into Lewis's booking on the *Royal Scot*, his suicide and the confirmation of his identity from articles left in the cabin; and from Dr Roche Lynch, who, as senior official analyst to the Home Office, was of the same opinion as Spilsbury and confirmed that both Maude and Freda had died from cyanide poisoning. Death, he said, would have been rapid and comparatively painless.

Did Lewis select his poison with care? Was cyanide his choice because it worked so speedily? One likes to think so. It may be recalled that during the war crimes trials after the Second World War both Himmler and Goering took cyanide in specially prepared capsules. Perhaps Lewis saw it as the kindest poison. How he administered it, however, would have presented him with a slight problem, for cyanide has a distinct taste. Possibly he administered it in a drink with a strong flavour. Only a mouthful of the drink would be necessary for it to be effective.

Was it long planned, this awful crime? The poison was purchased in early April. Had he nursed his scheme for six weeks? Or had the fish pond, recently begun and still not completed, unexpectedly suggested some awful possibility?

And what of the motive? Some writers have suggested that Maude was acid-tongued and that her ceaseless demands and nagging finally broke him. And Freda, according to some, joined in the baiting, but this is contrary to the view of those who knew Lewis and who spoke of a quiet man, one who never lost his temper. The previous Christmas, when he visited them, Frank Brown was struck by how happy and friendly the Lewises were. They seemed devoted to each other.

Perhaps whatever turned Charles Lewis into a double murderer lay not in his home but in his workplace. He had come to Erith from Wales in 1896 and had worked first in Erith schools and then for long years in the education office, where he worked his way up to Assistant Chief Education Officer. At the end, however, was there disillusion at how his career had come to a full stop when the ultimate post of Chief Education Officer eluded his grasp for the second time? Lewis was first passed over in 1903, when another local teacher, A R Flux, was appointed to the senior post. It was another 25 years before the vacancy occurred again after Flux died of a stroke. For two months Lewis ran the department until Frederic Evans came on the scene. Did natural disappointment over the years turn into corrosive bitterness? Did this sober man, who appeared to get on with his job in the face of disappointment, who seemed to take his failure to reach the top philosophically, secretly burn with resentment? And was his hurt, his envy, turned, not against his colleagues, but in some perverse way against his wife and adopted child? There is no way of knowing. It is only surmise.

More to the point, and likely to have had more influence on his actions, was the incomprehensible fact that Lewis had defrauded his employers, and there is some evidence that the authority's auditors were investigating the books in the days before the murders. They were eventually able to conclude that there had been some financial irregularity. The *Kentish Times* of 26th June 1931 reported that 'the thorough investigation that has taken place at the education offices since the tragedy has revealed a state of affairs which, if they do not occasion an alarm, do at least cause considerable anxiety'. In fact there was a discrepancy of

£600 in the accounts, enough to buy a decent house in those days. Lewis, of course, kept the Erith Education Department accounts as well as those of Kent County Council as far as these related to local expenditure. Did he know during that Whitsuntide holiday that within weeks he would be charged with embezzlement, that he faced a prison sentence? How could he face up to that? How would his wife and daughter respond? Did he fear that they would be deeply shamed because of his actions? This may be the true motive for the murders. Perhaps this was his way of saving his family from disgrace. Perhaps he came to believe that they should die in order to escape humiliation.

And the lack of logic in all this – the secret burial, the incoherent telephone calls, the letter to Wales, the passage to Leith and finally the suicide. It argues for a man driven to despair by the folly of his actions. Why did a modest-living man, conscientious and essentially decent, find it necessary to defraud his employer? Was it some kind of petty revenge for his lack of advancement? Can that have been it? And can it have led to the tragedy of 37 Erith Road?

THE ELTHAM
MURDER MYSTERY

————————❁————————

It was a tiresome beat out there, right on the edge of the Metropolitan Police area. Nothing much happened round sleepy Eltham, especially on this shift, which dragged its way across midnight and through the hours towards dawn. What could ever happen here, among these scattered farms and market gardens, along these hedge-lined country lanes? Kidbrooke Lane was as dull as anywhere else on PC Gunn's beat. Of course it was popular enough as a lovers' lane but not at this time in the morning, not at four o'clock, with the sky just beginning to lighten and the first birds and wayside animals coming out to join him.

Perhaps he ignored the faint whimpers at first. Perhaps he fancied they were the usual sounds of the waking world. But then, on the left side of the lane, he could faintly make her out, on her hands and knees, her head bobbing towards the ground. Drunk? Out here? Never! he thought. As he went to her he heard her moan, 'Oh, my poor head,' more to herself than to him. Then just as he reached her, just as he said, 'Here, take hold of my hand,' she fell to the ground. 'Let me die,' she groaned.

She was unable to give any clear answers to the constable's questions. Only when he shone his lantern on her did he see the horrific injuries to her face and forehead. In all there were a dozen incised wounds on the girl's face, one of which had almost torn an eye from its socket. Her jaw was fractured. The bone of the right temple was shattered, and from it brain matter protruded.

In the next hour or so, with the assistance of another officer, he managed to have the girl taken to Dr King in Eltham village. He thought that she could have been attacked no more than two hours earlier. That seemed to accord with PC Gunn's view, because when he passed along the lane at ten o'clock and later, just before two, he had not seen her. Even though it was dark he would surely have heard her. Surely he would not have missed her – not twice.

And so began that early morning, on Wednesday, 26th April 1871, what was to become one of Britain's most fascinating murder mysteries.

Later in the day the girl was taken to Guy's Hospital, where doctors said that she had been bludgeoned, possibly by a hammer, first by someone standing in front of her, and then after she had fallen to the ground. But it was not a sex attack; nor had it been a robbery, for there was money in the pocket of the victim's dress. Although for some days she was intermittently conscious, the unknown girl was never capable of speech and moved inexorably to her death on Sunday, April 30th. The post-mortem gave the cause of death as brain injury. She was two months pregnant, although the child in her womb had been dead for at least a week.

She was described as being 'respectably' dressed. Her hat was adorned with artificial pink roses and there was a rose motif on the lapel of her jacket. Her hands and knees, perhaps slightly calloused and roughened, suggested that she was in service.

Back at the crime scene, police officers noted footprints and 300 yards away saw blood on the stones by the brook. They concluded that the attacker had stopped there to wash himself. They were sure that he was a local, someone who knew the area, because instead of following Kidbrooke Lane to its extremity he had taken a short cut across the fields leading to Blackheath. A metal whistle, allegedly found some hours after the removal of the girl's body, was later to make its appearance in court.

On the Thursday there was what the police hoped was a major breakthrough. In the grounds of Morden College, more than a mile from where the girl had been attacked, they found a lathing hammer, a tool used by plasterers. With a 16-inch handle, its head was fashioned on the one side as a hammer and on the other as an axe. It was new, made by Sorby of Sheffield, and it was stained with blood, to which were attached some hairs. Only one ironmonger in the locality, Thomas's in Deptford High Street, stocked Sorby's hammers. The proprietor's wife, Mrs Jane Thomas, recalled that a short, black-bearded man in his late twenties or early thirties had purchased it some days earlier. She thought he might be a labourer, a jobbing gardener perhaps.

On the day after the girl died, William Trott, a Deptford lighterman, along with his family, turned up at the police station.

They had read an account of the girl who had been murdered.
The clothing described in the newspapers resembled that worn by
their niece. Shown it, they recognised the dark jacket with the
pink rose on the lapel. The Trotts were then taken to identify the
body. The face was so disfigured that at first a formal
identification was difficult. Only her nose, her mouth and a
mole on her right breast enabled them to name Jane Maria
Clousen.

The Trotts had seen Jane on the Sunday before she died. She
had called to have tea with them. It was her seventeenth
birthday. She had been excited, had seemed happier than she
had for weeks. Only a week or two earlier she had suffered
such a setback. On April 6th her employer, Mrs Pook, had
asked to speak to her. There had been gossip. She wanted to
know the truth: was Jane pregnant? Once Jane admitted her
condition, she was dismissed. But, last Sunday, Jane had had
news for the Trotts, news which, from what she said, she ought
not to have confided. For some time she had had a secret
romance with Edmund Pook, her former employer's youngest
son. He had given her a locket, she said. Now Jane told her
cousin, Charlotte, 'You must not be surprised if I am missing
for some weeks, for Edward says I must meet him ... on
Tuesday ... to arrange to go with him into the country. He says
he will have such a deal to tell me, and we shall have to make
all the arrangements. He says he is going to take me to a
christening with him at St Ives. Then we shall go to somewhere
else, to such a nice place, where I shall be so happy; but I am
not to tell anyone where I am going or write to anyone for
some time, as he does not want any one to know where I am.
You must not be surprised if you miss me for some weeks, but
you shall have the first letter I shall write to anyone. Edmund
says I shall not want for money, and if it's £5 I shall have it –
and I shall be so happy.'

The statement which Charlotte Trott made to Superintendent
Griffin and Inspector Mulvaney, the Metropolitan Police officers
responsible for the investigation, was corroborated by her mother,
who added that after the christening Jane and Edmund were to
marry secretly. No one, not even his family, would know until it
was all over. Both Charlotte and her mother reiterated that Jane
had said she was to meet Edmund on Tuesday at seven o'clock, at
the top of Crooms Hill in Greenwich.

Mrs Jane Prosser, another close friend of Jane Clousen, told the police that she too knew of the intended Crooms Hill meeting. Jane had also confided that she was 'in the family way' by Edmund. Intimate friend that she was, Mrs Prosser had never seen Edmund. No one in fact, not even the Trotts, had ever seen her in the company of the young man.

Mrs Fanny Hamilton of Ashburnham Road, in whose house Jane went to lodge after leaving the Pooks, said that she took a short stroll with her on the Tuesday evening. They left the house at about 6.30 and parted at 6.40, when Jane went off to meet Edmund at Crooms Hill.

Armed with this information, Griffin and Skinner visited the Pooks' comfortable double-fronted house at 2 London Street, Greenwich, on Tuesday, May 2nd. Ebenezer Pook was a printer and bookseller with a thriving business where he employed his two sons, Thomas and Edmund. There were three servants: a cook, a boy who did a variety of tasks and a new, trainee housemaid, Jane Maria Clousen's successor.

Griffin and Skinner met Ebenezer Pook first – presumably because his son was legally a minor – explaining to him that they were enquiring into the murder of his former housemaid. Then Edmund was summoned. He was a good-looking man, clean shaven, 20 years old, and he in no way resembled the man the police believed to have purchased the hammer. On being questioned, the young man said that he had not seen Jane Clousen since the day of her dismissal and he had not written to her. 'I know nothing of her,' he said. 'She was a dirty young woman and left in consequence.' Ebenezer Pook added that the girl had been unsatisfactory and that in the course of her almost two-year stay at the household had been warned a number of times about her unsatisfactory work. This was contrary to the opinions of other witnesses who described her as 'a clean, respectable, hardworking young woman' and a former employer at New Cross, who expressed his and his family's extreme satisfaction with Jane.

Asked about his whereabouts on the night of the murder, Edmund answered that he had worked every night the previous week till seven o'clock. 'On Monday night,' he said, 'I was about the town and on Tuesday I went to Lewisham and came back about a quarter past nine.' He explained that he had gone to Lewisham to see a girlfriend. Unfortunately he had not met her.

The policemen asked to see the jacket, trousers and shirt Edmund had worn on the Tuesday night. There were bloodstains on the left cuff of the shirt. Edmund explained that he had cut himself at work. The detectives were not convinced by this. On the trousers there were also what appeared to be bloodstains. Edmund explained that he suffered from frequent epileptic fits, during which he bit his tongue and bled heavily. His father and mother told the policemen that because of his fits he rarely went out by himself. They liked someone, his brother or an employee, to accompany him.

Edmund Pook was arrested, though without any concrete evidence, and later, at Greenwich Police Court, he was charged with Jane Clousen's murder and refused bail. It was as if a decision about Edmund's guilt had already been reached. Thereafter, and long before the trial began, the local newspapers presented their opinions to the reading public, whipping up public feeling against the accused man. In Greenwich the Pooks were jeered at in the street and snubbed by former friends and acquaintances. Their house was besieged by menacing crowds. Business suffered. Edmund Pook, transferred by train from Newgate to Maidstone prison, complained in a letter to his father that 'at every station on the line, as far as Dartford, there was a crowd of people ... who came to pass remarks upon me'. He believed that the stations were telegraphing each other to say that he was on his way. The story of the working class girl seduced and then murdered by a wealthy ne'er-do-well always played well.

Naturally, there was genuine public sympathy for the murdered girl. When she was buried at Brockley Lane cemetery, thousands lined the roads as the cortège passed by. But there was also a morbid curiosity. It was estimated that 20,000 people visited the scene of the crime on the Sunday after the murder. The police, meanwhile, were seeking firm evidence that Edmund had been in the vicinity of Kidbrooke Lane with Jane and of his having purchased the hammer. They were overwhelmed with the volume of information. Witnesses certainly came forward. Among them was Thomas Lazell, a gardener living in Kidbrooke Lane, who declared that he had seen Pook, his arm round a young woman's waist, walking across the cornfields at about 6.50 pm. William Sparshott, a Deptford ironmonger, claimed that Edmund Pook had called in his shop to buy a lathing hammer. Sparshott did not

Horrible Murder in Greenwich Outrages Citizenry

stock such a tool and said that he directed Edmund across the road to Thomas the ironmonger. Others spoke of seeing Edmund at about nine o'clock on the Tuesday night going into Mrs Playne's confectionery shop on Royal Hill, Greenwich, and here he brushed his clothes. He had been running and was 'hot and excited'.

It seemed that with these witnesses the prosecution had a good chance of success. Identification of Edmund, placing him at the Deptford ironmongery and in Kidbrooke Lane, was essential to the prosecution case.

Such was the strong feeling against Edmund that when the trial opened at the Central Criminal Court on July 12th, all the jurors were selected from outside Kent and Surrey.

One blow to the prosecution was the refusal by the judge, Lord Chief Justice Bovill, to allow hearsay evidence. What Jane Clousen was purported to have said to her relatives and friends about her pregnancy and her relationship with Edmund Pook was not to be admitted as evidence, the judge arguing that the accused could risk being convicted on the unchallenged story of a girl who could not be cross-examined about what she was alleged to have said.

When the evidence about the hammer was introduced, Mrs Thomas, for the defence, was adamant that she did not sell a hammer to Edmund Pook. He did not resemble the purchaser at all. Other witnesses in the shop were sure that the purchaser had been wearing light-coloured trousers. The defence produced evidence that the accused man did not possess any light trousers. Because of frequent bleeding as a consequence of his fits, he wore only dark clothes.

Walter Perren, by day a cabman and by night a music hall entertainer, claimed to have met Edmund outside Thomas's shop. He had seen him enter the shop and almost immediately afterwards saw Mrs Thomas reach towards a plasterer's hammer in the window. He was unable to confirm that she had taken it into the shop. But Perren's account was always suspect. He was introduced by the prosecution at a very late stage. Why had he not come forward earlier? Later he and another witness to the hammer story, James Conway, were charged with perjury.

Thomas Pook added weight to the defence by saying that on the night on which the hammer was bought he and his brother were in Greenwich all evening, except for 15 minutes when Edmund called in at the Literary Institution. It would have been impossible for him to go to the shop in Deptford and return in that time.

Thus the hammer evidence presented by the prosecution failed dismally.

Then other prosecution witnesses were ruthlessly demolished by the defence team. The testimony of Thomas Lazell, who had said that he saw Pook and Jane in Kidbrooke Lane at 6.50 pm was contradicted by Fanny Hamilton, a Crown witness. She had been with Jane in Douglas Street, Deptford, at 6.40 on the evening of the murder. This was nearly three miles from the murder scene. In addition, Lazell was challenged strongly over a conversation with a neighbour whom he had apparently told that he had seen no one in the lane on the night of the murder. William Norton and his girlfriend had heard shrieks at about 8.30 when they were in Kidbrooke Lane but they had thought them simply to be lovers playing. He later saw a man in dark clothing running back towards Shooters Hill Road but could not identify him. So much for strong identification of Edmund in Kidbrooke Lane.

So where was Edmund on the night of the murder? Thomas Pook again testified, this time telling the court that until 7.20 they were together, after which Edmund left for Lewisham. And again, at 7.25, Edmund called at the Literary Institute just for five minutes and was seen there by at least two witnesses. At Lewisham four other independent witnesses said they saw him leaning over the railway bridge at about 8.30.

Unknown to her parents, Edmund had been courting Alice Durnford of Lewisham for at least a year. The railway bridge on which he was seen was close to Miss Durnford's home. The only way he had of contacting her was by blowing a metal whistle outside her house. That night she had not heard the whistle. So Edmund gave up waiting and ran home. Supper was at nine o'clock and he was already late. Several witnesses saw him running down Royal Hill at about 9 pm.

But, asked the prosecution, had he not stopped off at Mrs Playne's shop, sweaty and breathless, to brush blood off his clothing? How could he account for that? He had fallen, Edmund said. He had slipped down in the gutter at South Street in Greenwich and went into the shop to brush the mud off his trousers. It was simply to conceal the fact that he had fallen from his mother, who worried about his health. She would think he had had another fit. In any case, the defence asked, would the killer not have been saturated with blood and anxious to get himself home rather than parade himself in front of witnesses?

Of course the whole matter of timing was a problem for the police. It is also a problem for anyone trying to blame Edmund Pook for the murder. If Edmund met Jane at 7.30, the earliest possible time they could have met, they had to walk nearly three miles to where she was murdered. Presumably their walk could not have taken them much less than, say, 60 minutes, possibly longer, for lovers dawdle. The earliest time that he could have killed her would therefore be about 8.30, the time that some witnesses heard shouts. Then the murderer had to wash himself in the brook. How long would that take, assuming that he was heavily bloodied? He then had to run back to Mrs Playne's shop and stay there for two or three minutes and be home by 9.15. Nearly three miles in 45 minutes – less washing and brushing time – is not impossible, but the path was hilly, rough and uneven all the way, with many stiles, two brooks, and some gates to negotiate. It is cutting it very fine, and the jury cannot have been convinced that the sickly Edmund Pook was capable of such exertion. Did he – could he – manage this nearly six-mile round trip in one and three quarter hours?

And the metal whistle, admitted by Alice Durnford to be similar to the one that Edmund used to call her, which had been found near Jane Clousen's body – what about that? This might have been a conclusive piece of evidence against the accused. Instead, it was a source of police embarrassment. They said that it had been found on the night of the murder. Then why was it not logged officially the defence asked. What was to say it really did come from the crime scene? What if it had really been found before the murder? Where were the details? What a flop.

After a four-day trial, the jury took 20 minutes to find Edmund Pook not guilty. It was a confusing and complex case, and there was no real alternative but to accept the guidance of the judge to acquit.

Superintendent Griffin and Inspector Mulvaney, against whom Ebenezer Pook was later to issue an unsuccessful writ for 'wilful and corrupt' perjury, were heavily criticised by the Lord Chief Justice for 'colouring the evidence'. He might well have criticised them for incompetence too. They certainly failed to prove their case. Were there no other possible suspects? Why did they not pursue the possibility that Jane was killed in the early hours, as the first doctor to see her suggested? The crime scene was unprotected and the footmarks were never measured before being obliterated by sightseers. The failure to log the whistle was a serious error. Hair found on the axe and on Edmund's trousers might well have been important, had not the defence successfully contended that they had been contaminated by being placed next to a lock of Jane's hair in the evidence bag. As for the locket that Jane had said was given her by Edmund, it was discovered to have been a gift from another Pook employee.

The acquittal of Edmund Pook was not well received locally. Mobs took to the streets. They had thronged Maidstone only three years earlier for the last public hanging in Kent and they still had the taste for expressing their ghoulish outrage. On the night of July 17th a crowd of up to 4,000 demonstrated outside the Pook family home. Days earlier effigies of a woman being attacked by a man using a plasterer's hammer had been paraded through the town.

The *Kentish Mercury* published libellous articles about Edmund. The Pooks felt obliged to take court action and received damages, but the family was to be tainted for long years. Some friends tried to raise funds for them, for they had been financially damaged by the cost of the trial, but these attempts produced little.

So who did murder 17-year-old Jane Clousen? Was she really pregnant by Edmund? Had they secretly planned to go away together as the Trotts said they had? Or was the girl just fantasising? Did she have some other, faithless lover?

In spite of his acquittal, Edmund Pook has been condemned down the years by eminent criminologists such as Colin Wilson, who have tended to ignore those many witnesses who attested to the fact that he was a very well-behaved and decent young man, who gave penny readings to illiterates. He has been described as unfaithful to his lady friends. Well, there was Alice Durnford of Lewisham and perhaps at the same time he was pursuing another girl, Alice Langley, at Deptford. But he was only 20 years of age. Such cavalier behaviour by very young men is hardly unknown.

But just supposing Edmund did murder Jane Clousen, how did he manage to get away with it? What exactly did happen? In spite of everything, the nagging doubts do persist. The mystery remains.

In The Night

———————— ❁ ————————

Believe it or believe it not, but this is the story. It is the sheer ordinariness of this family which makes the story so curious, for they have had their lives turned over, ruined some might say, in the most remarkable way. Or at least that is what they say has happened and they have had significant and strong support for their claims from scientists, doctors, social workers and psychiatrists. Whether you believe them or not, theirs is an arresting tale, the subject of searching enquiries and many articles.

Paul and Ann Andrews and their young sons, Daniel and Jason, lived at Sweetbriar Cottage at Slade Green. Each day, Paul and Ann went off to their ten-acre smallholding, Hawksnest Farm at Crouch, to attend to their livestock.

As far back as 1989 the Andrews had difficulties with their animals. Quite unaccountably, they lost twenty-two calves and seven sheep all at once, and this completely baffled the vets. Then something even odder occurred. They received a phone message purporting to come from a Ministry of Agriculture official. Contrary to the usual procedure, they were told not to incinerate the carcasses on this occasion. Within days the carcasses were taken away by six men wearing protective clothing and gas masks. The Andrews were told that they were not to use the land for grazing for the next 12 months. After that time they would be given clearance to return it to use. After 12 months, not having heard from the Ministry, Paul Andrews rang them but no one knew anything of the matter. There was no official collection service: carcasses were always burnt. The Ministry was as baffled as Paul and Ann Andrews.

Then animals were found mutilated. A horse had a large flap cut in its shoulder. There was very little sign of bleeding. The incision, according to the vet, was deliberate and he pointed out where the tissue below the skin had been removed. But why? And why, on another occasion were six horses, including a foal, found, each with a bloodless wound on a hind leg? In August 1986 Paul found four dead mice laid out in a line near the farm gate. Each had a small hole in the forehead, the left eye missing and the rectum cut out. In 1995 the farm cat was found dead with a hole in its head and later a fox was found with the same fatal injury. It was suggested that the brain and the spinal cord had been removed via the hole. So, scenes of dreadful mutilation and all apparently completely inexplicable.

This is very mysterious and there are those who claim it to be a sure sign of extraterrestrial experimental activity. On the other hand others regard the whole matter as evidence of cruelty to animals, though no one has ever accused the Andrews of any responsibility for this.

But if the mutilations are inexplicable even more so are the allegations of alien intervention into the life of the Andrews family. 'The most extraordinary tale of alien abduction ever' was how *The Sun* described their plight in its four-day serialisation of 'The True Story of Alien Abduction in Rural England', by Jean Ritchie, a highly respected journalist who had spent months with the family.

Right from Jason's infancy there had been odd happenings. One night when he was four years old, there was a furious hammering at the front door. When Paul went to answer there was no one there and no one in the road outside. As he turned to go back into the house there was a deafening clap of thunder and a streak of lightning seared the sky. At that point Jason, who had been sleeping on the sofa, woke up and immediately began to speak, the words spewing out, the language complex and interspersed with huge numbers, strange algebraic formulae, and abstract terms used by mathematicians.

Now the banging on the door began once more and the whole cottage shook: its walls, its doors, its windows. In alarm Paul tried to telephone the police but the telephone was dead. Then, just as suddenly as it had begun, the noise and shuddering of the house stopped, and Jason stopped speaking. Now the little boy stood up, walking towards the door as if in a trance. Paul made to catch hold of him. Where was he going, his father demanded. 'They are waiting for me,' the child shouted, struggling to free himself. 'I have to go.' Again the knocking began and just as suddenly subsided. At the same time Jason came out of his trance. At last Paul was able to summon the police, who listened to his story, perhaps with some doubt, as they could find no sign of damage to the door or to any part of the house.

Over the years there was a series of other baffling occurrences. The electrical appliances – the TV, the radio, houselights, for instance – would come on quite unexpectedly.

Jason became a constant worry to his parents. Sometimes when he got up in the morning there was mud on his pyjamas and on his hands and legs. Was he sleep walking, his parents wondered. Sometimes there were scratches on his body, sometimes even more angry scars, which seemed to disappear quite quickly. There was the time when Jason was taken to a doctor in Maidstone. On his body there was a six-inch scar which Ann had never seen before. A week later it had disappeared just as other scars had come and gone. In school Jason's behaviour was disruptive and he received counselling from a psychiatrist. It was a dozen or so years after the first odd occurrences when, one evening in 1995, the Andrews family were watching a TV programme about a man who could not account for two and half hours as he was driving home from work. What had happened to him in this missing time? He said that since then he had suffered from acute depression and mood swings. At this point, with the programme still showing, Jason, now 12 years old, stood up and with tears pouring down his face shouted at the screen, 'That man there is stupid. He should be glad he can't remember. He should leave it like that. Because I remember. I remember everything. I'm scared. They won't leave me alone. Why can't they leave me alone?'

They? The light comes on first, the distressed boy tells his parents. It is usually about three o'clock in the morning and he always knows in advance when they are coming because his head tingles. 'Then I see the tall one rise at the foot of the bed.' The tall one is about five feet four inches tall, Jason tells his astonished parents. He has a large head, large slanting black eyes and a small nose and mouth. And there are several smaller figures too. When they arrive, Jason cannot move. He tries to shout for his parents, but they never answer, never come to help him. And later he finds himself in a cold, all-white operating theatre. He cannot speak, cannot move. And though he sees the tall alien touch him, he never feels him. And there is an operation but with no knives – only long, slender fingers. 'I hate them,' Jason shouts. 'I hate you for not coming when I need you. Why do you let them take me?' This has gone on for years, he tells his parents, ever since he was an infant.

He recalls the first visits, the long fingers picking him out of the cot. In his time, he says, he has met aliens both tall and short, kind and sinister, some with huge round eyes, others either light-skinned or dark-featured. He says that they communicate through telepathy and that when they arrive they have the power to paralyse the rest of the family, to make them incapable of action.

Was the boy talking rubbish? His parents must have wondered, but now Daniel explained that he too had had strange things happen to him. He remembered visits by aliens to his room when he was small but when Jason was four years old they had transferred their attention to him. And now, on the nights when they come to abduct his brother, Daniel tells how he lies in his bed, incapable of movement. He recalled that only the previous night he was wakened by a bright light and then felt as if something had entered his body and taken possession of it.

From now on Ann and Paul set out to learn all they could about alien visitations and abductions. They read everything available on the subject, attended UFO conferences, immersing themselves in the topic. They were convinced that aliens were regularly abducting their son. It seemed to Paul and Ann that the incidents in Jason's childhood were now explained; aliens were at the root of them all.

Reflecting on her own childhood and past, Ann was now convinced that she too had been abducted, although she was unable to recall the precise details, and that possibly her father and even her grandfather had been abducted. Had her family been targeted, abducted and monitored across the generations? It seemed so. She claimed that on one occasion she had seen a head, larger than a human's, behind a tree. It was pale, hairless, with an almost luminous quality about it. Was she still being monitored? Even Paul, initially more sceptical, concluded that there was something in this. He began to agree with Ann that they were under surveillance, though not solely by aliens, but also by men in black, from the densely wooded MOD property which skirts the smallholding.

For Jason, who hated his experiences, there seemed to be no escape. He went on holiday in a mobile home at Allhallows with his mother and two friends. But the aliens came in the night. Distressed, he told his mother, 'I didn't think they'd find me here; not on holiday.' In the early hours of the next morning there was a disturbance in the living room. On investigation, they found that

Hawksnest Farm with dense woods beyond.

furniture had been moved, and on the window pane was the image of an alien's face.

Back at home some time later, Jason woke screaming one night. He had dreamt that Honey, one of their horses, was dead, and the next morning at the smallholding they discovered that the dream was true. According to the vet, the animal's stomach had simply exploded and it was now impossible to suggest the cause of death.

Ann now felt herself to be more closely involved with the aliens. One night she woke to find the bedroom flooded with white light, but then fell straightaway into a sleep. The same night Jason was abducted, waking in an enormous room along with scores of other people. They had looked at a giant screen, showing the earth blowing up. Was this a message to the people on earth? Jason, describing the scene, recalled seeing his mother in the crowd. It was all the proof that Ann needed. She too, she knew, had been abducted the same night. Nor was it the first time. She remembered now that one night her bedroom was filled with light and then she found herself near the smallholding, three miles from home, still in her nightclothes. She was in a clearing and saw a horse staggering to its feet as if it had been sedated. It was her own stallion, Cardi. The horse wandered off into woodland ... and Ann woke up in her own bedroom – a curious dream, she thought – but later in the day Ann met a local woman leading a horse in the lane outside their house. It was Cardi. He had been found wandering in the woods, half dazed.

So complex and alarming had their lives become that Ann and Paul sought help and contacted Tony Dodd, a former policeman and now a leading investigator into alien abduction and mutilation. Dodd himself claims to have been a lifelong abductee, chosen to pass on messages, which he says he receives telepathically. He admits that the experience of abduction is terrifying. The aliens mean no harm, he says; indeed, he believes them to be benevolent, seeking to help mankind against future, more malevolent aliens. Nevertheless, he fears them. He says, 'It's easy to be calm and rational in the cold light of day but when night comes so does the fear. Having seen their craft and awesome power, I know we can never stop them.' One simply has to accept these things: 'How do you fight something that can paralyse you, then levitate you and then float you out of the house through the walls?'

But he believes that Jason is special, a chosen one, who has been selected for multiple abductions and that the aliens will probably follow him all his life. Jason accepts the possibility of this, though he admits to feeling suicidal at times. 'Perhaps I have been chosen,' he says. 'Perhaps I am special. Maybe one day I will understand. But now I'd just like it to stop. I want them to let me be ordinary.'

Is any of this believable? Thousands subscribe to the notion of alien abduction. Many reputable scientists and many highly placed military staff throughout the world subscribe to the idea that this is more than delusion or hoaxing. They are convinced by the sheer volume of reports, the common features of so many independent accounts and the physical and emotional responses of so many who claim to have been abducted. Many like Tony Dodd insist that there are government cover-ups in all of the major countries of the world, that governments keep secret what they know about these advanced alien societies. Those convinced of alien activity suggest that animal mutilation is to test for toxins on living creatures.

In the course of his work, Nick Pope, a former UFO desk officer at the Ministry of Defence Secretariat (Air Staff), amassed what he asserts is alarming evidence about UFOs, aliens and abductions. Abduction by aliens is fact and not fiction, he says. In Pope's view it is not the invention of cranks and attention seekers, nor does he subscribe to the cover-up theory. Governments in his opinion are simply ignoring the truth. He says, 'This phenomenon needs serious investigation. The real crime against humanity may not be that inflicted upon us by extra-terrestrials, but rather the official indifference that allows the phenomenon to continue unchallenged.'

Some researchers now are suggesting that these aliens do not necessarily originate from outer space. They are proposing that the UFO phenomenon perhaps relates to other dimensions of our own world.

But – now to focus on the sceptics – should we accept these tall tales? Kevin McClure, who has studied the whole business of alien abduction for many years, concludes that it is all fantasy and myth, often sincerely held by gullible people. Why, he has asked, were the animal killings and mutilations reported in Dodd's various writings, and in the book by Jean Ritchie, never looked into at an official level? He sees them as criminal acts. And why were Jason's disappearing scars not more closely investigated? Does a boy who has felt suicidal not merit closer consideration? McClure believes the ideas propagated by Ritchie and Dodd are capable of damaging the psychological health of vulnerable people.

Then there are the conclusions of Dr Susan Blackmore, Professor of Psychology at the University of Manchester. She believes the simple truth to be that many alleged abductees have hallucinated as a result of the effects of electromagnetism on the temporal lobes of the brain. Or take the more down-to-earth views of James Dalrymple of the *Daily Mail*. After *The Sun* ran its four-day spread, Dalrymple interviewed Jason and came away dismissive of the whole business, describing it as mumbo-jumbo. He did not believe the Andrews family to be more than harmless obsessives, highly suggestible people who misguidedly believed in the possibility of alien abduction. His view was that they all became such converts that they began to attribute to alien intervention every minor incident and each unaccountable act involving their younger son, and indeed the animals on the smallholding. Like McClure, Dalrymple was deeply concerned about Jason, who had little to say at the interview and whose answers he considered were prompted by his mother and Jean Ritchie. 'I had a bad feeling about Jason,' Dalrymple wrote. 'He is now locked for ever into his role as Britain's most famous alien abductee.'

Other voices, however, speak out loudly for the Andrews, convinced by their assertions that they are alien abductees.

Believe it or believe it not, that is their story.

THE GUNNER'S
STORY

——————— ❁ ———————

Rodney Pattenden was in his back garden making up the greenhouse fire at about 9.40 that October night. When he first heard the screams he thought it was a nightbird of some kind but when he heard the bang against the front gate he ran to investigate. A woman was lying there motionless, and then he saw the overturned pushchair, the little boy still inside it.

He could just make out that the woman was hurt. He picked up the child, took him inside the house and called the doctor. But it was too late for the doctor to do the woman any good. She had been stabbed fatally in the neck. The police were called to 'Valhalla', the Pattendens' house in Brompton Farm Road. They identified the victim as 35-year-old Ellen Symes, a married woman, five months pregnant, who was a close neighbour of the Pattendens. Both families lived in the same road. Mrs Symes' house, 'Thames Mount', was on the other side of the crossroads.

The police quickly established that the murdered woman's husband was on night shift and that she had been out visiting her parents. It was a routine that on Fridays she walked up to Dickens Terrace to see them and that they walked back part of the way with her, usually as far as the Wainscott Institute, which was not far from her home. It was safe enough here, despite the blackout. It wasn't dangerous like the towns in this open countryside.

This particular evening, 9th October 1942, Ellen Symes and her parents parted company at the Institute at about 9.30. Mr and Mrs Overy called in at the Institute while their daughter went off with the pushchair, expecting to arrive home in ten minutes or so. By the hedge on the other side of the road from 'Valhalla', she was attacked. There was a trail of blood from the hedge to the gate, 30 yards away. The dying Ellen Symes, whose screams Rodney Pattenden had taken for a nightbird, staggered across the road, still pushing her four-year-old child, until she slumped heavily against the gate.

It was four-year-old Robin who provided the first useful piece of information about the crime. He knew enough to say that his mother had been attacked by a soldier.

On the Saturday morning, only 12 hours after the murder, a soldier was stopped by a policeman in Gravesend Road on the outskirts of Strood. He admitted that he was absent without leave and was taken to the police station at Rochester. He was a Gunner in the Royal Artillery, Reginald Sidney Buckfield, a former labourer from Mansfield and a married man with three daughters. For three months or so he had served with Battery 542 at Oak Tree Camp on Dallywood Road. Then, a fortnight earlier, he had been posted to an anti-aircraft battery at Tollgate, Gravesend. He had gone absent on September 26th, spent a day in Paddington, where he had seen his wife, and then returned to the area he now knew quite well. Since then he had worked at local farms as a fruit picker. At Whitebread's Farm in Wainscott he had worked for a week and later he had found similar work at Benuncle Farm, Hoo, and at Larkin Hill Farm. He made about ten shillings a day, enough to enable him to eat breakfast and tea in local cafés and bars and to visit Bates the barber for a shave every day. At night he slept rough. This, then, was Reginald Buckfield, known to all and sundry – farmers, barmen, soldiers – as Smiler for the sole reason that he constantly smiled; in good times and bad, whether the going was easy or not, he smiled. Perpetually.

Asked at Rochester Police Station about his movements the previous evening, he answered that when he finished work he had had tea opposite the Majestic Cinema in Rochester. Then he had played billiards at the Seamen's Mission. After that he went to the Steam Engine pub in Station Road.

The police now took him in a car around the area which he said he had visited the previous night. Buckfield guided the driver from the Steam Engine to The Ship, and then along Bill Street Road and Lower Rochester Road, and down Dallywood Lane to its junction with Gravesend Road. Just past the Oak Tree Camp, he pointed to some stacks of straw. 'That's where I slept last night,' he said. 'I spoke to Bombardier Perrett at ten o'clock at the top of the lane.' He was careful throughout the tour to say at what time he was at particular locations.

Reginald Sidney Buckfield.

Back at the police station, his fingerprints were taken, his fingernails examined and hairs pulled from his head. His uniform was also taken from him and exchanged for other clothing. Not unreasonably, he began to ask questions. On the Sunday morning he said to a constable, 'There's something fishy here. I'm being held for something more than being an absentee. They don't take your fingerprints and pull your hair out for that. Do you know what I'm being detained for?' The policeman was non-committal. 'It seems funny,' Buckfield said. 'Every time I break out, something always happens, either a break or a murder. I've already been interrogated.'

Later in the day, Chief Constable Kenneth Horwood, to whom this remark had been reported, interviewed Buckfield, who said to him:

'You must be keeping me for something more than being an absentee.'

'What do you think I might be keeping you for?' the Chief Constable asked.

'I've been interrogated for three before,' the soldier replied.

'Three what?'

'Three murders.'

'But I haven't mentioned murder to you.'

'No, but there must be something in it, as you've examined my hair and my hands. I've tried to find out from your man, but no one will tell me.'

Buckfield explained that six months earlier, in early March 1942, he had been arrested as an absentee in Staffordshire and at the same time questioned about murders in London and Southport. He was never charged, and whether there was any substance to this mysterious matter is not known.

Now, at the Chief Constable's request, Buckfield wrote an account of what he had done on the Friday evening after leaving the Steam Engine. After this he was shown a bone-handled table knife, the blade of which had been sharpened to a point. It had been discovered two hours after his arrest in the orchard of a house about 100 yards from 'Valhalla'. The soldier claimed not to recognize the knife, saying that the last knife he had was a jackknife, which he had sold a fortnight earlier.

On the Sunday, Buckfield was told for the first time that a woman had been murdered about 300 yards from where he had slept on the Friday night. He said that he had not seen a woman and child that night. Buckfield was given no further details of the crime.

After four days, with no substantial evidence to charge him, Buckfield was released into military custody to be charged with desertion. As he left Rochester Police Station, he handed 13 sheets of paper to a detective. 'There you are, officer,' he said. 'Read them very, very carefully. You'll find them very interesting.' And true enough, they were very interesting. In fact they are among the most remarkable documents ever to be presented in court. In his cell Buckfield had begun writing on the evening of October 10th what he was to describe later as 'all fiction'. When he left Rochester, his 'fiction' was not complete but it provided enough material to be absorbing for the police and the court.

Entitled 'The mystery of Brompton Road by Gunner Buckfield', it suggested that its author knew more about the murder of Ellen Symes than any innocent man ought to. Innocent only of the rules of spelling, punctuation and the practice of regular fiction writing, Buckfield wrote his manuscript over three days, and there is no doubt that it was a guilty man's attempt to suggest that he had an alibi – the details of his earlier written statement to the police were not dissimilar – and that there were other people to whom the police ought to pay attention.

The story is told for the most part in dialogue, principally by Smiler in the third person, although at other times the text reverts to the first person. Only nicknames and abbreviations are used for the other characters such as Pop and Bert, the latter resembling Alfred Symes, who is made to appear jealous of his wife. There is also the mysterious stranger, towards whom suspicion is directed. Another suspicious character is the cyclist whom Smiler asks for a light. The manuscript contains a number of vital references to the actual events of the evening. The edited version, sparing the reader Buckfield's insecurity with the surface features of the written language, starts as follows:

'Detective Office, Rochester.
Copy of document written by Reginald Sidney Buckfield.
The Mystery of Brompton Road by Gnr Buckfield
    'Hello, Smiler.'
    'What a bloody night!'
    'Not so bad,' Bert replied.
    Smiler: 'You coming in for a drink?'

'Well, I don't mind if I do get out of this wind and darkness.'
'What's yours?' said Smiler as they entered the bar.
'Well, I dunno,' said Bert. 'I fink I'll have a pig's ear.'
'OK. Two pints of nine, guvnor.'
'Coming up, Smiler. What's the weather like outside?' the
barman asked as he handed the drinks over and took the money.
'Bloody cold and dark,' the two cockneys said at once. And the
remark was passed by a cheeky chappie that it was a 'luverly
night for a murder, guvnor'.
Laughter!
'You know, my old china plate, there is many a word said in
jest that comes true. Ain't that right, Smiler?'
'Yes, I suppose so.'
Now let us weigh these two men up. Starting with Bert, so
called. He's a married man, got a wife and one daughter; his job is
doing night work round Strood or Rochester. He's a happy-go-
lucky sort of guy, cares for nothing, lives along the Brompton
Road somewhere or, shall we say, near it. His wife and child are
happy-go-lucky, so that makes the merry-go-round. Now we will
drop Bert for a while and go to Smiler, a soldier in the RA,
stationed somewhere in England, but as it happened at the time an
absentee ... The ways of Smiler were happy-go-lucky, full of life
and laughter ... One would say he wasn't the type of man that
girls will go crazy over, but wait and see; as this story carries on,
you will be surprised that he turned out to be a true Bluebeard.'

Note that Ellen Symes' husband lived 'along the Brompton
Road' and in real life had a wife and a son rather than a daughter.
He also was on 'night work round Strood or Rochester'. And
what about Smiler's being 'a true Bluebeard'? Does he mean
simply a ladies' man? Or something worse?

Later in the story Bert says his wife is visiting her parents but he
does not worry about her being out alone. He says, 'Her mother
and father see her to the bottom [of the road] and the rest of the
way she comes home on her own ... My wife always gets in just
before 10 pm or 9.30 pm.'

In chapter five, the narrator, now referred to as 'I', writes: 'I
made tracks out of the pub just at 8.10 pm, and reached another,
called the Ship Inn, at 8.30 or 8.35 pm; stopped till 8.50 to 8.55
pm ...' (This is similar to the written statement he made to the
police.) He continues, 'I made tracks towards Dallywood, got

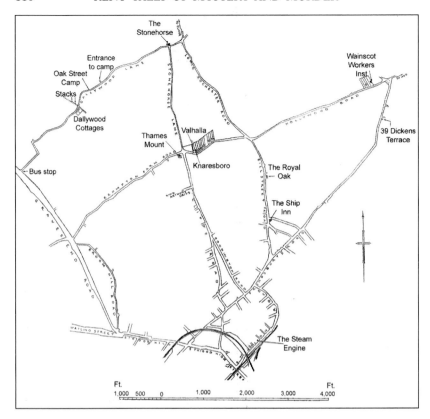

Plan used at the trial of Buckfield.

settled down after all these little things were done by me at 10.15 pm. The little things mentioned are: I stopped and asked for a light below the Royal Oak, which would be 9.5 pm, off a civilian with a cycle; he never had such; I walked on towards 542 by Stone Horse on Cliffe Road, looked in Stone Horse, carried on to outside battery gate, stopped there for five or ten minutes, time being 9.20 or 9.25. Knowing Miss X [his former girl friend, Kate Harmer] was out, I decided to wait for her at bottom to come off bus, got to bottom at 9.30, saw bus. Sailor and civilian girl turned down Dallywood. Didn't move till asked for a light by a bombardier from Battery 542.'

And so it goes on, but here, in a supposed work of fiction, is his entire evening – every crucial minute – accounted for. Even the interrogation in Rochester Police Station is included. The Chief Constable speaks at one point and says, 'Three hundred yards from where you slept, Gunner X, a woman was found murdered, and the funny part about it is that you were in the vicinity at the time it was committed.' It becomes difficult to tease fact from fiction, fiction from fact. But how did Buckfield know so much? On the Sunday he had been told that there had been a murder but nothing more. When he wrote his manuscript he was confined in a police cell. How much had he been able to glean about the murder during the time there? None of the men on duty said anything to him about the murder. He saw no newspapers. Challenged about this, this least likely of literary men told a detective, 'It's how I thought the murder might have been committed. I've written stories before, you know.'

While in military custody at Chatham, Buckfield was questioned several times by civilian policemen. On one occasion he was told that another soldier, James O'Hara, recognised the knife, now accepted as the murder weapon, as similar to the one that Buckfield had used to pare an apple at Benuncle Farm three days before the murder. Buckfield had responded angrily, 'It's a confernal lie. I never had a knife. Let me face him and have it out.'

After he was formally charged at Rochester on November 7th, Buckfield introduced a new witness into his defence. He had seemed to be well covered as far as his alibi was concerned. He was undoubtedly seen at ten o'clock at the junction of Dallywood Lane and Gravesend Road by Bombardier Perrett and other witnesses, including his former girlfriend, Kate Harmer. But now he feared that he had not sufficiently covered the time around 9.30 pm. And so he now recalled seeing ATS Private Kathleen Parfitt, who worked in the officers' quarters at Oak Tree Camp, in the lane at 9.30. She had been with a friend. She had been pushing a cycle. Miss Parfitt was found. Yes, she had been in Dallywood Lane at 9.30 with a friend. They were returning to camp after a night out in Rochester and, yes, she was pushing her cycle. This was so far from the scene of the murder that if Miss Parfitt agreed that she had seen him at that time, he would be a free man.

During his Old Bailey trial in January 1943, Buckfield was challenged about introducing this late witness. Why had he not mentioned her in his statement? Why did she not appear in his 'fiction'? 'Well, I was rushed so much that it absolutely slipped my memory,' he said in answer to the prosecuting counsel's question. But was it not strange, he was asked, that he had mentioned two total strangers, a sailor and a civilian girl, who, incidentally, had never been found? And wasn't it equally strange that he had twice omitted to mention his former girlfriend?

But Miss Parfitt had not seen Buckfield that night, she told the court. She had not seen him for a fortnight. Had Buckfield simply guessed that she would be there in Dallywood Lane at that time.

The sharpened knife appeared to be a strong piece of evidence against Buckfield. Certainly the police laboratory proved that the blood on it matched that of Ellen Symes, but at the trial the witness O'Hara was now less certain than he had seemed, saying that he thought Buckfield's blade tapered more and that it was lighter in colour than the one produced.

Another witness, farm labourer William Gutteridge, told the court that the knife was certainly similar to that used by Buckfield at Larkin Hill Farm the day before the murder but Gutteridge was not very precise. The knife shown him now, he said, was 'a similar knife as what I see; it ain't far off neither', but under cross-examination he asserted, 'I never said it was the same knife.'

With the unwillingness of these two witnesses to identify the knife more certainly, the defence might have found a loophole. But then Buckfield ruined his case by insisting that he had not had any knife for a fortnight before the crime. This very much told against him, as did his insistence that the knife now presented in court was not the same knife that they had brought to the Magistrates' Court. It was absolutely futile to take such an absurd stance.

As to the 'fiction', the jury was obliged to hear it read aloud in the courtroom. Mr L A Byrne, for the prosecution, knew that it was his most powerful piece of evidence. How could it have been written without first-hand knowledge of the murder? 'Did you know when you began to write this story,' Byrne asked, 'that the murder had taken place in Brompton Road?'

'Oh no,' answered Buckfield.

'If that is so, can you tell me why you headed the first chapter of your narrative, The Mystery of Brompton Road?' Buckfield floundered and the judge felt obliged to repeat the question in different words.

'Well,' the accused man said, reaching for an answer, for any answer, 'I was thinking of London at the time, my lord – of

Brompton Road.' Mr Justice Hallett was little impressed with this answer.

'A very disastrous thing, wasn't it, that you should have, out of all the tens of thousands of roads in London, selected the one road that happened to have the same name as the road where the murder had happened?'

'Well, it seems that way, my lord, yes.' After that could anything be believed that Buckfield said?

Buckfield was found guilty and sentenced to death. He still smiled. But when passing sentence the judge made a significant comment. The guilty man's constant smiling had suggested to him some mental imbalance. 'As is usual,' said Mr Justice Hallett, 'investigation will be made by the proper authorities as to whether there is any medical explanation of your act.' Within days, Buckfield was reprieved, declared insane, and sent to Broadmoor.

At the trial, the prosecution counsel was to remark about Buckfield's work of 'fiction': 'It is the composition of a man who had the most intimate knowledge of the movements of this woman.' How would he know about her? This is simply a guess. He was a cheerful, outgoing sort of man, the kind of man who spoke to anybody and everybody. Perhaps during his posting at Oak Tree Camp, he had passed Ellen Symes with her child in the pushchair. If he did see her, he was likely to have started up a conversation, telling her about his home in Nottinghamshire, his wife and his three very young daughters. She in reply would perhaps have told him about her husband, about being a local girl who visited her parents on Fridays – not that this explains why Buckfield should then murder her, but it may explain why it was that he knew so much of her background. This is not to suggest that they had any liaison; that seems to be out of the question. But possibly they were the slightest of acquaintances. It is possible that on the night of the murder their paths crossed quite by chance, but what triggered off the violent attack on Ellen Symes can never be known.

ABC

———————— ❊ ————————

It was a lorry driver going up Shooters Hill who spotted it first, saw something lying in the road. Most drivers at one o'clock in the morning would have given it no more than a cursory glance, but our man was sufficiently curious to stop his vehicle and climb down from his cab. Then as he walked towards the bundle, it stood up and made off into the woods. It was like a cat, he was to say, but bigger than any cat he had ever seen. Anyway, he was impressed enough to report his sighting to the police. Shortly afterwards another motorist reported that he too had seen the animal. So they sent round a policeman, just to check. And there it was, still on the outskirts of the wood, bold as brass, in the early morning light. No, the policeman reported to his sergeant, they weren't making it up. It was a cat all right, a big one, too – better seal the woods off; better warn the locals as well. And later didn't it turn up again and leap across the bonnet of the police car?

They said that it was a cheetah, that animal seen entering Castle Wood, Eltham, in the early hours of Thursday, 18th July 1963. The sighting started one of the biggest police hunts ever seen in Kent. They were aided by soldiers from Woolwich garrison as well as by boys from Shooters Hill Grammar School, and others. On they went, sweeping through 100 acres of woodland but with never a sighting of their prey and no clear indication of what they were to do if by chance the animal had hung around long enough to be cornered.

The *Eltham and Kentish Times* catches some of the feeling of an expedition in its report: 'While a real holiday atmosphere prevailed in lovely Castle Woods at the weekend, and children and visitors from all over London made Shooters Hill a temporary tourist resort, nagging fear has persisted in the minds of the police, who still watched the woods, that reports of a wild animal lurking there might even now prove to be true ... Police and troops were replaced by holiday makers and sightseers, children with sticks and bows and arrows who daily joined in the hunt for what was thought to be a cheetah.'

At night police officers with walkie-talkie radios and tracker dogs continued to patrol Castle Wood, Jack Wood and Oxleas Wood, but like the daytime hunters they never caught sight of it.

Was it really a cheetah, this creature slinking through the woods? Or was it some supernatural phenomenon? Some wondered whether it was the spectral black dog, that grim manifestation which has haunted so many areas of the country over the centuries? Was it some creature like Black Shuck, which wanders the lanes of East Anglia? Was it similar to Yorkshire's ghostly Guytrash? Was it the Wish Hound from southern England? Or the black dog that haunts the Pilgrims' Way? Was this some vestige of the hounds of legend? Or was it the remnant of some ancient stock, from times long past, hidden for generations in woods and moorland and unsuspected till now?

Real and mysterious cats had been known about for years, long before the 1960s. There are odd stories from times past told in remote parts; there are records of shootings and sightings over a hundred years ago, but it was not until the 1960s that the story of the mystery cats took off. The eventual acknowledgement of the existence of unidentified cat-like animals haunting Kent and other parts of Britain came only after several years of tentative enquiries and vague reports from uncertain and embarrassed members of the public. Each year now there are sightings in Kent – about 20 in 1998; 36 in 2000.

Fortean Times, that marvellously idiosyncratic collection of curious data and sceptical conclusions, has been monitoring the situation throughout the United Kingdom since 1964, for Kent is not alone; all parts of the country have had their cat-like visitors, their so-called alien big cats, their ABCs. They have appeared in various parts of Scotland, the Fens, in East Anglia, and pretty well everywhere throughout the United Kingdom. There is the beast of Bodmin and the Durham puma. The Pentlands in Scotland have their own mysterious panther and in Yorkshire there is the Beast of Broomhill. There is a creature seen around Norwich and others at Aberystwyth and on Exmoor. There is the Surrey puma, and inevitably that haunted spot, Blue Bell Hill, has lent its name to the ABCs seen in its vicinity over the years. Some ABCs maintain a permanent reputation – the Surrey puma, the Beast of Bodmin – as though they were sole and unique representatives in their area, but there must always be more than just one cat carrying the title.

The most common ABCs reported in the United Kingdom are

the black leopard and the puma. There have been fewer sightings of the lynx and equally few of the smaller ocelot and jungle cat. Most witnesses speak of a large black or dark brown cat – commonly referred to as a 'black panther' – about the size of a labrador between 18 and 30 inches high, with a body two to four feet long and a long tail. The puma tends to have a yellow coat, sometimes with faint stripes or spots. Perhaps too there has been some inter-breeding, and some sightings of black cats the size of a fox are referred to as 'black hybrids'.

In increasing numbers ABCs, especially lynx-type animals, are reported going about their business. In 2002 there were nearly 500 sightings in the UK. They are on our roads, in our meadows, and in our forests. Their business is to survive: to feed themselves and their young, and to find good, safe, cover. Simple enough. So they seek out foxes, domestic cats, chickens, geese, lambs and rodents. They lead their essentially private lives in woodlands and heaths. On occasion, in their continuous search for food in their territory, they cross our paths and even, though more rarely, enter our territory.

In the last dozen years, from which most of the examples cited come, ABCs have been seen more frequently. In Marden some years ago a man rang the police; there was a puma in his garden. At Snodland a resident reported that a big cat had made a hole in his garden hedge and was on the lawn. Someone at Allington reported a puma prowling in his garden. A motorist driving with his family in the Sevenoaks area one evening spotted a large black leopard crossing the road only 25 feet or so ahead of him. It then walked up the pathway at the roadside, its eyes glowing green. In the early hours of the following morning, a van driver near Bluewater saw a panther – at least he described it so – crossing the road only six feet away from his vehicle. One early afternoon in January 1998 a passenger in a van saw a black leopard as it crossed a field. In February 2001 Christine and Raymond Pearson of Fawkham, driving on the B255 between Bean and Crayford, saw a big cat, which jumped off the bank at the side of the road and ran across, straight in front of their car, into a field on the opposite side. Mrs Pearson said, 'It had a flat coat which was dark fawn in colour, like a mountain lion or a puma. The animal was about two feet high and three feet long.' At Crayford in June 2001 Paul Fountain of Farm Place saw a sandy coloured puma in his front garden.

They are great leapers, these animals, great climbers too. In

April 1998 at Strood a sandy coloured cat leapt 12 feet from one roadside bank to the other in Stone Horse Lane. A month earlier at Hempstead a big cat was seen stalking lambs. But when it became aware of a human nearby it leapt into a tree and then down into the undergrowth to make its escape.

On rare occasions the cats are seen quite relaxed, sunbathing or lying asleep even. In May 1998 a sandy coloured big cat, accompanied by what might have been a lynx and even more improbably by a domestic cat, is alleged to have been seen sitting on a roof near a car park behind Allders in Chatham.

Not surprisingly, for these animals will follow their nature, they will attack livestock. Throughout the county in the last ten years there have been reports of slaughtered sheep. At Bridge, Mersham, Wrotham Heath, Boxley and several other places flocks have been savaged.

It seems likely that within 20 years or so there will be an explosion of such felines. As frequently opined by the media, who are always ready to raise the pulse with an opinion, whether tested or not, they are highly dangerous, and yet no spontaneous attacks on humans have been recorded. The Gravesend man clawed possibly by a lynx in February 1998 was trying to prise a live rabbit from its jaws. He had mistaken the animal for a fox. Many a domestic dog would respond as sharply in similar circumstances. According to the record, ABCs are not aggressive towards humans unless provoked, cornered or injured.

But where are they from, these silent cats which proffer us so few glimpses of their presence? Some undoubtedly have escaped from private menageries or zoos. Moreover, what does seem clear is that many animals – panthers, pumas and the like – which were kept as exotic pets were released into the wild after the passing of the Dangerous Wild Animals Act. This was introduced in 1976 and aimed at reducing the number of dangerous wild animals in private hands by compelling owners to license the premises where the animals were kept. Some of those unable to afford the licence turned their animals loose. Others applied to zoos to take their animals but they were turned away in their hundreds. Many owners, unable to bear the thought of having their pets put down, felt that release into the wild was the kindest option, although of course it cannot have been. Most of the animals, unable to fend for themselves, would simply have died, but those which survived created a viable breeding population, and it is these animals and their progeny which are seen today. The Countryside and Wildlife Act of 1982, which made it illegal to release into the wild any non-indigenous animal, came six years too late.

So what, if anything, is to be done? Look back at the response to the appearance of the cat at Shooters Hill in 1963. The soldiers, the holiday makers, the schoolboys, were out to do – what? What if the animal had been cornered and had turned on one of them? What then? What if in its response it had not only clawed someone; what if it had killed someone? No doubt there would have been an out-and-out, knee-jerk slaughter of the animals. They would have been classified as highly dangerous, public enemies, to be wiped out.

There are mixed views about the numbers of these animals and the dangers they pose. In 1997 it was reported that Malcolm Dudding, the founder of the Big Cat Foundation, claimed that he had never over many years seen paw marks or droppings which suggested that any big cat was living wild in Kent. Some sightings were in his view simply large domestic cats. On the other hand, the late zoologist, Quentin Rose, who devoted many years to the study of ABCs, feared that these predators represented a mounting danger to wildlife and farm stock. They might, he said, if shot at and wounded, attack humans and might even get the taste for human blood. For his part, Neil Arnold of Kent Big Cat Watch believes that the ABCs are now full-time members of the environment and ought to be protected. In August 2002 Arnold made a three minute film of a lynx to add to his other filmings of a black leopard and a golden cat. Di Francis, another big cat researcher, suggests that elderly ewes ought to be staked out in adjoining fields, reasoning that this stratagem would save younger, more valuable animals. And she is of the opinion that the death will be quicker and more humane than the trip to the slaughterhouse. Do such diverse opinions suggest the need for debate, direction, or government intervention?

But governments dither. In 1998 Elliot Morley, a parliamentary undersecretary, told Parliament that most, if not all, big cat reports were due to misidentification. 'Many allegations and comments have been made for many years,' he said, 'and none have been substantiated.'

Who is right?

THE LUARD CASE

———————❖———————

Someone commits a murder. It is a horrific murder. A 58-year-old woman is shot twice in the head, and, when her body is found, the costly rings she wore are no longer there.

The murder in the lonely wood at Seal Chart – the area in which it was committed – is not simply a great Kent mystery; it is one of the great unsolved British murders, a true classic, and in the years since it happened the identity of the murderer has puzzled crime scholars.

Follow up the rings for a moment. They are really quite valuable. Three of them are family heirlooms. One has a large diamond in the centre, surrounded by eight smaller diamonds; another is a twin setting of sapphire and diamond; the third has a large opal. The fourth is a solid gold band wedding ring. Yet they never turned up in a jewellers. What is the point of stealing jewellery with such savagery without then trying to sell it? This has intrigued many who have studied the case.

And what about this? The woman is in lonely woodland, and presumably her attacker is confident that he can safely rob her. But why does he murder her? Can he not deal with her in some other way, some less final way? According to some, it smacks of a revenge killing. If it is a robbery, it must have been planned; it cannot be on the spur of the moment. Can he – or she, or even they, come to think of it – be hanging around a wood on a Monday afternoon in the hope that some rich middle-aged woman with expensive jewellery on her fingers will turn up? Or perhaps it's just some opportunist – a man with a gun, some footloose desperado – who meets the woman by chance.

These are just preliminary thoughts to mull over as we go deeper into this intriguing murder.

The principal players in this late-Edwardian drama are the Luards, he a retired Major General, now a pillar of the community as a county councillor, magistrate and churchwarden; and she, highly thought of in the district, dedicates herself to good works. Apart from fulfilling the obligations and duties of people of their class, they live relatively quiet lives at their substantial home, Ightham Knoll. Here they employ a cook and two housemaids; nothing ostentatious, just what might be expected, at the time, of minor rural gentry.

On the afternoon of Monday, 24th August 1908, with their Irish terrier, Scamp, the couple take a stroll together, setting off from their home at 2.30 pm and walking through the nearby woodlands of the Frankfield Estate, which belongs to their neighbours and friends the Wilkinsons. They often take this walk with its promise of entrancing views from the summer house. Today, however, they have no time to dawdle. Caroline Luard must be back at the house by four o'clock, as Mrs Stewart, the wife of a local solicitor, is coming for afternoon tea. They stroll beyond the summer house, shaded by pine trees and surrounded by thick bracken. Minutes later, they reach the wicket gate at the exit from the woods. It is three o'clock and now Caroline turns back, retracing the ground she has already covered and going in the direction of the summer house. Her husband, with the dog, continues on his way to Wildernesse Golf Club at Godden Green. He has to collect his clubs from there because the next day they are going away to stay with friends. He will need to take his clubs with him. After all, a man cannot play decently well with borrowed clubs.

The general did not linger at the golf club. He returned home by the road. On the way, a local clergyman, the Revd. A B Cotton, out for a spin in his car with two ladies, stopped and offered him a lift. Luard declined, saying that he would prefer to walk back, but he was grateful when Cotton took his bag of golf clubs. Later the clergyman passed again and this time the general did accept a lift. According to the Revd. Cotton, his passenger was perfectly normal in his manner. They reached Ightham Knoll at 4.30, where the general, doubtless embarrassed, found his wife's guest, Mrs Stewart, waiting. The general took over as host and they had tea, presumably speculating all the while on Caroline's non-arrival. They wondered whether she had stayed at the summer house, rather fancifully named The Casa. It was, after all, one of Caroline's favourite places, high up on the ridge, a place where she often sat admiring the sweeping views. It was a substantial enough building with several rooms and a verandah. But at the moment The Casa was locked up as the owners were away. And, in any case, would she quite suddenly have forgotten her afternoon tea guest?

Eventually General Luard and his guest set off for the woods, although Mrs Stewart went only part of the way before returning home. Making his way up the winding woodland path, the general reached the secluded summer house. There he found his wife lying face down, a large pool of blood from two gunshot wounds spreading a foot on either side of her head. Her white blouse was drenched with blood. One of her gloves was found nearby.

Desperate, the general ran for help to the nearby cottage of the estate coachman, Fred Wickham. No, Wickham's wife would not do, he gasped, nor would his 19-year-old daughter. He needed a man. He went on to the stables and there found Wickham. In the end, after phone calls to the police and doctors at Sevenoaks, Harding, the butler at the Frankfield Estate, accompanied the deeply distressed general back to the summer house. It was now about six o'clock.

When Dr Mansfield arrived at 7.45 p.m., it was almost dusk. The body was cold, although as yet rigor mortis had not set in. Caroline's face was a mask of blood. Black powder-burns from the two shots to her head indicated that she had been hit at close range. One bullet had entered the cheek below the left eye. A second, behind the right ear, suggested that it had been fired from behind while she was lying face down. There was a third injury to the back of the head, although how this was caused was unclear.

Night shadows fell and the local policemen, Superintendent Taylor and Sergeant Paramour, searched the area round the summer house, the scene lit by motor lamps from the doctor's car and candles from the summer house, which had been opened. Caroline's body was placed temporarily on a camp bed in one of the rooms and later it was conveyed home in a horse-drawn fruit van. What the police did discover was a third bullet, in the ground in front of the verandah. They also noted that the pocket of the murdered woman's dress had been cut away and the small purse she had carried in there was missing.

Dr Mansfield was joined by Dr Walker and they completed the post-mortem at Ightham Knoll. Their only disagreement was over the cause of the third injury to the head. It was possibly caused when Caroline fell to the floor of the verandah after the first shot.

Major-General CE Luard and Mrs Caroline Luard.

Alternatively, it might conceivably have been caused by a blunt instrument.

Over the next day or so, the police scoured the wood, but the ground with its thick covering of pine needles yielded no clues – neither footprints, nor bloody tracks, nor a discarded weapon. They questioned people in the locality and there were references to mysterious strangers: an eastern gentleman; a black man, who was said to have admitted killing a woman and now wanted to find the railway station; a sandy-haired man seen on the Seal road by the Revd. Cotton that Monday afternoon. There were stories of tramps and itinerant hop-pickers, and on the evening of the murder a shady-looking character allegedly called for brandy at a public house in Larkfield and, agitated and trembling, offered a ring for sale. But none of these led to any result.

The Chief Constable of Kent called for assistance from Scotland Yard and Chief Inspector Scott and Sergeant Savage were sent to help. They had bloodhounds out searching the wood, but the scent was now three days old and there was no firm success, although the dogs picked up a trail, which seemed to confirm, as the Kent constables had suggested earlier, that the killer went south and east towards the Tonbridge road, using the thick bracken to conceal his movements.

The time of the shooting on that quiet summer afternoon was less difficult to pinpoint. There is little doubt that Caroline Luard was shot in the head with two .320 calibre bullets at 3.15 pm. Mrs Anna Wickham, the coachman's wife, in the garden of her cottage at the edge of the wood, no more than 350 yards from The Casa, heard three shots at that time. The first, she thought, sounded somewhat dull as if it had hit against something hard. After that she heard two more shots. Mrs Wickham had turned to her daughter Edith. 'They mean to kill that thing well at any rate,' she had said. She was able to confirm the time with confidence when asked and was certain that the shots she heard came from the direction of the summer house. Daniel Kettel, a gardener on the estate, also heard the shooting at 3.15, but he thought little of it; it must be someone shooting squirrels, he had thought. And some woodcutters reported hearing gunshots. In fact, one of them reported hearing a faint squeal before the first shot, but there was nothing surprising in that; it sounded like a rabbit being caught by a weasel.

Could the general have shot his wife? This was a question that the police inevitably, though reluctantly had to ask. But it was ludicrous. Would a man of 69, married to a woman for 33 years, suddenly murder her? Perhaps in anger, but not in this curiously calculated way, by taking her to the woods and then, having killed his lifetime's companion, making his way to the golf club. Would he then go through the whole business of returning home, giving tea to Mrs Stewart and engaging himself in all that followed? Impossible, surely, but the question had to be faced.

The general's alibi was unshakeable. He had left his wife at the wicket gate at three o'clock and leaving the wood, he went along Church Road as far as the junction with Stone Street. Turning right here, along the narrow winding road to Seal, he made for the golf club and at 3.20, at least a mile and a half from the summer house, he was seen passing the fir trees at the entrance to Hall Place by Thomas Durrant, a brewery manager. He cannot have travelled such a distance in five minutes. Durrant's assessment of the time was more or less confirmed by two other

The Luards' home, Ightham Knoll, in 1908.

witnesses. Five minutes or so later, Ernest King, a charcoal burner, had just checked his watch, when he saw the general further along the road to the golf club, and at 3.30 Harry Kent, the golf club steward, saw him at the clubhouse. It is a cast iron alibi and to this day it has not been broken.

Naturally the police retraced the general's route and found the timing exact. Superintendents Fowle and Taylor of Sevenoaks police walked over ground covered by the general and their times coincided exactly with his. They agreed. If the witnesses – at least, eight people – were correct, it was physically impossible for the general to have shot his wife.

The police admitted to being totally baffled. Their quarry had escaped without leaving the slightest sign of his passing. It is hardly surprising, then, that the inquest was adjourned on two occasions, there being so little of significance to report.

But the murmurs were deafening; the letters came in volumes, for people like matters to be tied up. Crime fiction is so neat and tidy. It always produces a villain and it punishes him. Not so with real-life crime. So, after the strenuous but unsuccessful efforts by the police to find the murderer, many of the public found it necessary to find their own conclusion to the story. Rumour fed on rumour. It was General Luard who had murdered his wife. This is how the story concluded for so many, and they wrote to the police, the coroner and his jurymen to tell them so. They also wrote to the general informing him of their verdict. Forget his alibi. Somehow he had managed to deceive the police with his timings. Forget the fact that none of the three revolvers he kept in the house was the murder weapon. Forget that he was a defeated, woebegone, old man. He was guilty, guilty, guilty. So considerable was the volume of poison pen letters, mostly anonymous, that Julian Symons in his book, *A Reasonable Doubt*, suggests that it resembled a concerted campaign against the general. By whom? By the murderer?

Deeply grieving, General Luard sold up his home and went to stay with a friend, Colonel Charles Warde, MP, of Barham Court, Maidstone. On the morning of September 18th, when he was expected to meet his son, Charles, returning from his regiment in South Africa, the general threw himself in front of a train at Teston. His body was cut in two. He had left a letter for his host. It read:

'My dear Warde
I am sorry to have to return your kindness and hospitality in this way but I am satisfied it is best to join her in the second life at once, as I can be of no further use to anyone in this world of which I am tired and in which I do not wish to live any longer. I thought that my strength was sufficient to bear up against the horrible imputations and terrible letters which I have received since that awful crime was committed which robbed me of my happiness. And so it was for long, and the goodness, kindness and sympathy of so many friends kept me going. But somehow, in the last day or two, something seems to have snapped. The strength has left me and I care for nothing except to join her again.
So goodbye dear friend.
Yours very affectionately
C E Luard
PS I shall be somewhere on the railway line.'

'Suicide while temporarily insane' was the verdict on the general. The verdict on his wife's death was returned as 'murder by person or persons unknown'.

Or may we call this two murders?

Over the years, a variety of names have been offered as the murderer of Caroline Luard. Some have continued to point the finger at Luard, in spite of his impregnable alibi. They have suggested that an innocent man would never have committed suicide and so burden his only son with a double death. Others have said that the general was given the tip-off from the Chief Constable that he was about to be arrested and, rather than face that, he took his own life. Not surprisingly, this story was denied by the police.

At the inquest on General Luard's death, the Chief Constable of Kent said: 'The police have ascertained beyond any doubt that there was not the slightest foundation for those rumours or accusations made against General Luard.' The jury added the following rider to their verdict: 'With your permission, Mr Coroner, we wish to enter a most emphatic protest against those persons who have written or forwarded anonymous letters to various members of the jury, with a view to influencing their minds and we shall hail with pleasure any action which may bring them to justice.'

There have been attempts to link the murder of Caroline Luard with John Alexander Dickman, hanged two years later for shooting a colliery wages clerk on the Newcastle–Alnmouth train. There were rumours that Dickman had defrauded Mrs Luard. When she took the matter to the police, so the story goes, he shot her. But there is no solid evidence to link Dickman with this crime.

In his excellent booklet, *The Seal Chart Murder*, published in 1995, local historian Monty Parkin, tells how the story still echoes faintly round the district, not that anyone now can offer much more than second-hand accounts. A few offer childhood memories. Some told Parkin that the general was still suspected. Others came up with tales of tramps and out-of-work labourers. There's mention of the general having had an affair with another woman or his wife with another man.

Another candidate for the role of murderer is the mentally unbalanced son of Sir William Boord, who lived opposite the Luards at Oldbury Place, Ightham. This young man usually stayed in a mental home but at the time of the murder he was living at Oldbury Place. It is said that on the day of the murder he was in a seriously uncontrollable state and that Dr Walker, who that evening with Dr Mansfield carried out the post-mortem on Caroline Luard, was sent for. Perhaps that is so, but it still does not place him in the wood with a revolver. Did Walker entertain doubts about his patient's actions on that day? If he had had serious concerns, he surely would have mentioned them to the police.

Then there was David Woodruff, a tramp who was charged with the crime in September 1909. He had been arrested at Bromley on a charge of assault and was found to be carrying a revolver, but it was not a .320 calibre weapon, the kind which had been used to shoot Caroline Luard, and the magistrates concluded that there were no reasons for proceeding against him.

So we are left with the same questions that we began with. We are no nearer resolving the case than were the Scotland Yard and Kent policemen almost a century ago.

Hazarding a guess – just a guess – as to the culprit? Well, it could have been some obscure, out-of-work labourer, perhaps a hop picker, a man criminally inclined and armed with a cheap and easily available gun, who, hanging about the wood with no plan in mind, met quite by chance an obviously well-off woman wearing classy jewellery and his attempt to rob her was resisted. So he murdered her, tearing the rings off her fingers. Then he crept through the undergrowth and out onto the Tonbridge road. And then went – where?

An unsophisticated solution? Absolutely, but no better, no worse, perhaps, than any of the others.

Bibliography

Andrews, Ann, and Jean Ritchie. *Abducted: The True Story of Alien Abduction in Rural England*. Headline, 1998

Browne, D G, and E V Tullett. *Sir Bernard Spilsbury: His Life and Cases*. White Lion, 1976.

Burridge, D. *Ley Lines and Church Alignments in East Kent*, Bygone Kent, 1980

Fabian, Robert. *Fabian of the Yard*. Cedar Books, 1956.

Fido, Martin. *The Chronicle of Crime*. Little Brown, 1993.

Gaute, J H H and Robin Odell. *Murder 'Whatdunit'*. Pan, 1984.

Hambrook, Walter. *Hambrook of the Yard*. Robert Hale, 1937.

Paine, Brian, and Trevor Sturgess. *Unexplained Kent*. Breedon Books, 1997.

Parkin, A M. *The Seal Chart Murder*. 1995.

Price, Harry. *Poltergeist over England*. Country Life, 1945.

Roberts, C E B. *The Trial of Reginald Sidney Buckfield*. Jarrolds, 1944.

Simpson, Keith. *Forty Years of Murder*. Harrap, 1978.

Spiller, Margaret. Articles on Pook-Clousen case in *Family Tree Magazine* and *North West Kent Family History Society Magazine*

Symons, Julian. *A Reasonable Doubt*. Cresset Press 1960.

Taylor, Bernard, and Stephen Knight. *Perfect Murder*. Grafton, 1987.

Timpson, John. *Timpson's Leylines*. Cassell, 2000.

Watkins, Alfred. *The Old Straight Track*. Abacus, 1925.

Noseweek (issues 25, 26)